STUDY GUIDE

NEIL T. ANDERSON

the CHRIST

DISCOVERING AND ENJOYING YOUR

CENTERED

FREEDOM IN CHRIST TOGETHER

MARRIAGE

CHARLES MYLANDER

FOR PERSONAL USE IN INDIVIDUAL, COUPLE
OR SMALL GROUP SETTINGS

Gospel Light

PUBLISHING STAFF
William T. Greig, Publisher
Dr. Elmer L. Towns, Senior Consulting Publisher
Dr. Gary S. Greig, Senior Consulting Editor
Jill Honodel, Editor
Pam Weston, Editorial Assistant
Kyle Duncan, Associate Publisher
Bayard Taylor, M.Div., Editor, Theological and Biblical Issues
Debi Thayer, Designer
Lisa Guest, Contibuting Writer

ISBN 0-8307-1889-3
© 1997 by Neil T. Anderson and Charles Mylander
All rights reserved.
Printed in U.S.A.

Contents

Preface

Never before in our history has there been such a concerted effort to save the family. All kinds of helps are available to achieve stronger, longer-lasting, more intimate marriages, and yet we're not winning the battle! Simply trying to force proper behavior in relationships really doesn't work, even among Christians! Resolving the deeper inner conflicts most people experience must happen first, then proper behavior will follow, resulting in successful relationships.

This study guide is about walking in the light. It's about getting radically right with God. It's about becoming all that God created you to be. When that happens, there's great hope not only for you but for your marriage.

A WORD TO ENGAGED COUPLES

If you're engaged or thinking seriously about marriage, you're to be commended for taking the time and effort to work through issues in your life that need to be brought to light. *The Christ-Centered Marriage*, along with this study guide, will take you step by step through the process of deepening your relationship with God as well as with your future spouse.

In the appendix of this study guide, you will find Beginning Your Marriage Free. It has been modified from the Steps to Setting Your Marriage Free and is intended to be used by those contemplating marriage. It will help you identify dysfunctional patterns which have been ongoing in your family for generations. No one is perfect. No one was raised in a perfect family and no one marries into one either. However, you can take the necessary steps to gain your freedom from the strongholds in your life now before you marry, and you can learn how to deal with the issues that will crop up in your marital relationship as you grow in Christ and with each other.

How to Begin

Whether you are working through this study guide to strengthen your marriage or in preparation for marriage, we strongly encourage you to *first* work through the individual Steps to Freedom in Christ which can be found in the appendix of *The Christ-Centered Marriage*. Other resources that may help you through this process are *Victory over the Darkness*, *Victory over the Darkness Study Guide*, *The Bondage Breaker*, *The Bondage Breaker Study Guide* and *The Steps to Freedom in Christ*. These are available in most Christian bookstores or from Freedom in Christ Ministries.

If you have trouble working through these steps on your own, be sure to ask for help from your pastor, a Christian counselor or fellow believer. Before you can have marital freedom, you must find your personal freedom in Christ.

Once you have successfully processed the individual Steps to Freedom in Christ, you are ready to begin the study guide.

Tips for Individual Study

We encourage you to read *The Christ-Centered Marriage* and work through this study guide as a couple. Each spouse should have his or her own study guide. There are a number of ways to do this study. The following are suggestions to help you develop your own plan:

- Set aside one evening a week to read one chapter and answer the questions in the study guide together.

- Read one chapter through the week a little each day as a devotional and then complete the corresponding study guide chapter separately. Set aside a time later in the week to discuss your answers.
- Go away for a long weekend to a quiet place without distractions and do the whole study, or break it into a couple of weekend sessions a few weeks apart.

If you are working through this inductive study alone, you need to focus on your own responsibility rather than your spouse's. The book emphasizes that each spouse must assume his or her own responsibility to meet the needs of the other person. Marriage cannot flourish as God intended if each spouse refuses to take responsibility. In the absence of cooperation, we encourage you to remain faithful and to do your part for your sake and the sake of your marriage (see 1 Corinthians 7:12-14). It is neither your right nor your responsibility to change your spouse, but by changing your own attitudes and actions you will become the husband or wife that God has called you to be. No one but yourself can keep you from becoming the person God wants you to be and fulfilling His will for your life.

In the process of reading *The Christ-Centered Marriage* and this study guide, many other questions may arise. There is a place at the end of each chapter to write your own questions for further study, for group interaction or to ask your pastor, group leader or counselor.

The optional *Christ-Centered Marriage* video series is available to give you further guidance. One video introduces each chapter, and another guides you through the process of setting your marriage free. Both videos could be used by couples alone, in Sunday School classes, small groups or discipleship ministries.

TIPS FOR GROUP STUDY

Because much of the material in this study guide is personal, the leader will need to be mature in handling the group. It would be counterproductive for the leader to probe into the group members' personal lives during the group time.

This study guide is ideal for marriage seminars and retreats. It takes several hours to successfully process the Steps to Setting Your Marriage Free. Each step could be started in the group setting with the couples completing the step at home. When we conduct this process as a marriage seminar, we plan for two hours on Thursday and Friday evenings, and then meet for eight hours on Saturday, allowing for breaks during the eight hours. This process has very little lecture and a lot of individual couple interaction. Therefore, it is important that the setting have adequate facilities so that couples can have privacy during their times of interaction.

In preparation for group discussion, invite couples to use the space provided at the end of each chapter of this study guide to formulate any questions they may have. These questions can be used for group discussion.

Obviously the group study will not be as effective if everyone has not read *The Christ-Centered Marriage* book that goes with this study guide. We encourage you to make the commitment to each other to read the book together. The benefits to your marriage will have eternal results.

THANKS!

We want to thank Lisa Guest for writing this study guide. She has proven herself to be gifted in this area of ministry.

And we thank you for taking the time to make your marriage the best possible. May God bless you and keep you together in Christ.

Neil and Chuck

Introduction

The Christ-Centered Marriage

To maintain a Christian marriage we have to become one in Christ.

- As you begin this study, spend a few minutes together discussing the following questions:

Why have you picked up *The Christ-Centered Marriage* and this study guide?

What do you hope to gain from reading this book?

- During the second half of this century, a cultural revolution has taken place in this country. Marriages, families and the Church have been dramatically affected by it.

In what specific ways have the Nifty Fifties and Shocking Sixties impacted you—your personality, your values, your history, your marriage?

What concerns you most about today's culture and, specifically, its impact on marriage and the family?

- Programs, retreats, as well as books and tapes by James Dobson, Gary Smalley, Norm Wright and countless other marriage and family resources are available today. Excellent biblical instruction for family disciplines relating to God, society, marriage and parenting are readily available.

What other resources have you benefited from and how have they helped?

- A couple struggling with their marriage sometimes seeks counseling, but in some cases the counselor's plan of action has little or no effect. It is not that most Christians don't want to behave appropriately. In many cases they can't because of unresolved internal conflicts.

How did you react when you first read that diagnosis?

Do you agree with it? Why or why not?

Many Christians struggle in their marriages. What unresolved internal conflicts are an issue in your marriage?

- As you think about your marriage, look again at the Marriage and Family Spirit-Controlled Disciplines wheel that has Christ at its center.

Marriage and Family Spirit-Controlled Disciplines

Spiritual

Conversion · Family Devotions · Prayer · Communication · Discipline

Parenting Training **Christ** Bonding **Marriage**

Sports · School · Family Outings · Work · Sex

Social

DIAGRAM I.2

Which spokes have you worked to strengthen?

Which spokes are weak?

What are each of you doing to stay connected to Christ, the hub of the wheel, and to keep Him at the center of your marriage?

What are you and your spouse doing together to abide in Christ?

What challenge(s) do you find in the introduction to *The Christ-Centered Marriage*, especially in the last section (pp. 18-19)?

Read together the closing paragraph of the introduction on page 19. What hope do you find in this paragraph?

QUESTIONS FOR FURTHER STUDY OR GROUP INTERACTION:

NOTES FROM GROUP INTERACTION OR PERSONAL COUNSELING:

God's Perfect Design

*Relationships are the heart of life, and the relationship
between the male and the female is the earthly expression of the relationship between God and humankind.
But it is only in Christ that our marriages can become
what God intends them to be.*

- Let's begin by considering God's perfect design as He
  originally intended it.

What new insight or timely reminder about God's plan for us,
His created beings, did you gain from the sections
"Companionship—A Universal Need" (pp. 22-23) and "An
Eternal Need" (pp. 23-25)?

What about this big-picture context is especially helpful or
encouraging to you?

What clearer understanding about your marriage covenant did you gain from the discussion "A Covenant Relationship" (pp. 25-27)?

What sentences stand out in this section that may be a message to you from God?

• Read again Michael P. Horban's "Marriage License—A Learner's Permit" (pp. 27-28).

What sources of frustration in your marriage are opportunities for self-sacrifice?

As a way of loving your mate, what about him or her do you need to stop trying to change?

What good has your spouse brought out in you?

What do you think you need to change about yourself that would improve your marriage relationship?

- Consider now the three essential criteria for a successful marriage. The first criterion is leaving Mom and Dad.

In what ways have you not left your mother and father—physically, emotionally, mentally, spiritually and/or financially?

Are you still seeking your parents' approval? Consider the following questions and support your answers with specific examples of things you have or have not done.

Does the approval of relatives (or others) mean more to you than the approval of God? If so, why?

In what ways are you still trying to live up to the expectations of your parents or other family members?

Is your relationship with God the most important relationship in your life?

If you answered yes, then what about your life demonstrates that your most important relationship is with God?

If you answered no, what in your life needs to change to make your relationship with God the most important?

How can you demonstrate to your spouse that your relationship with him or her is second only to your relationship with God?

Have you ever severed any other relationship that threatened your relationship with God or your spouse?

Are there any relationships right now that threaten your relationship with God or with your spouse?

What do you need to do to sever those relationships?

What family heritage and patterns of personal behavior have you brought into your marriage that are not conducive to a stable marriage relationship?

As parents, what are you doing now to prepare your children to "leave and cleave" when they marry?

If you are a parent of adult married children, what—if anything—are you doing or expecting that may interfere with or even weaken their attempts to leave and cleave?

- The second essential ingredient for a successful marriage is oneness of soul and spirit as well as body.

What do you and your spouse do to overcome the ordinary as well as the extraordinary demands of life that make it difficult to bond?

How often do you and your spouse pray together?

What, if anything, is keeping you from being totally committed—body, soul and spirit—to your spouse?

What evidence *do* you see in your marriage that God is making you and your spouse one?

• A successful marriage also requires intimacy and transparency. The husband and wife need to have no unresolved issues between each other or between themselves and God.

What do you see in yourself that is blocking intimacy and transparency?

____ Unforgiveness?	____ Unconfessed sin?
____ Skewed priorities?	____ Busy schedules?
____ Laziness?	____ Something else?

What are you doing and what will you do to remove the blocks you've identified?

Are you willing to work toward intimacy and transparency in your marriage? Acknowledge your willingness before God and your spouse.

There are times when working toward resolving your own personal and spiritual conflicts has helped when marriage counseling has been unable to help. Pray about whether that is advice for you right now, and as you do, ask God to make you the kind of spouse who is willing to share, willing to forgive and willing to accept your mate, warts and all.

QUESTIONS FOR FURTHER STUDY OR GROUP INTERACTION:

NOTES FROM GROUP INTERACTION OR PERSONAL COUNSELING:

The Curse of the Fall

The fact that we are products of our past and that the sins of our ancestors affect us and our marriages are theological issues. We must biblically understand this fact if we are to embrace Christ as the center of our marriages.

• Unless we make concentrated efforts to reprogram our minds and retrain our habits, we will bring into our marriages all that we have been taught in the past.

What did you learn, both good and bad, from your parents' marriage about how spouses relate to each other?

What unhealthy thinking and unhelpful patterns of behavior that you learned from others will you have to work at preventing so your own marriage relationship will not be adversely affected?

- The cosmic spiritual battle that began with the Fall affects the social, the physical and the spiritual realm that we live in today. Apart from Christ we are simply products of the past, subject to the consequences of the sins of our ancestors, leaving us and our marriages void of purpose and identity.

Spiritually dead, Adam and Eve struggled to find their identity and purpose for living in the natural world. How have you witnessed humanity putting its hope in the natural realm as it struggles for identity and purpose?

Because neither Adam nor Eve had a relationship with God as a result of the Fall, they were faced with the question of "who should rule?" How has the struggle over who should rule been troublesome in your marriage?

This chapter traces Satan's attempts to interfere with God's redemptive plan and His advance of the messianic line. In what ways have you observed Satan still trying to interfere with God's redemptive work? Explain your answer.

- The messianic line is an important Old Testament theme, thus the burning question: When would the child be born to carry on the redemptive line? At one point Abraham and Sarah were no longer willing to wait for God's timing.

Read Genesis 15:1-7; 16:1-15. How did Abraham and Sarah try to force God's hand?

What were the tragic consequences of their actions?

What legacy have their efforts to help God left us even today (see also Genesis 21:1-21)?

In what ways are you taking your marriage into your own hands rather than trusting God?

What lesson does God want you to learn from the experiences of Abraham, Sarah and Hagar?

- Marriage is not unrelated to the cosmic struggle between God and Satan. All of creation has been affected by the Fall. As a result, godless bloodlines (illustrated by Ahab and Jezebel) and the iniquities of our ancestors impact every one of us in some way.

The Old Testament recognizes that the iniquity of the father is visited upon his children (see Exodus 20:5; Deuteronomy 5:9). Such sins, iniquities (a rebellious spirit or strong self-will), and idolatry must be confessed if generational sins are to be broken. What sins, iniquity and idolatry are you aware of in the lives of your parents, grandparents and great-grandparents?

Have you confessed them even if they haven't? If not, do so now.

Like people in the times of Jeremiah and Ezekiel, we are guilty of downplaying individual responsibility and crediting our own weaknesses to the failings of others, especially our parents and the dysfunction of our families. Where are you blaming rather than taking responsibility for your own attitudes and actions?

Saints in the Old Testament dealt with generational sin and corporate sin as well as individual personal sin by repenting. Define repentance.

For what do you need to have a "change of mind"? What do you need to acknowledge as sin (see Romans 3:23) and to renounce (see 1 John 1:9)?

- Our churches and marriages will experience tremendous turmoil if we enter into those relationships with a saving knowledge of our Lord Jesus Christ without any evidence of repentance.

Repentance is incomplete unless we give up our sinful habits, traditions, customs and meaningless religious practices. In what areas of your life has repentance been merely a matter of words rather than actual changes?

How will you behave differently now that you have repented?

Having repented and renounced your sin, what do you need to do to receive the gift of forgiveness and eternal life? See Romans 3:23, 1 John 1:9 and John 3:16.

Having repented, renounced and accepted by faith God's forgiveness made available through Christ's death on the cross, note Paul's instruction in Romans 12:2—"Do not conform any longer to the pattern of this world, but be transformed by the renewing of your mind." What are you doing to open yourself to God's transforming touch that will renew your mind?

QUESTIONS FOR FURTHER STUDY OR GROUP INTERACTION:

NOTES FROM GROUP INTERACTION OR PERSONAL COUNSELING:

Christ First

*The order of Scripture is to first present every person
complete in Christ, so our marriages and our families
can be whole and functional again.*

- Marriage is the first institution God created, but the whole
  can be no greater than the sum of its parts. God must be
  first and foremost in the lives of both mates for the marriage to thrive.

Read Matthew 10:34-39. Did you notice that no mention is
made of bringing a sword between the husband and the wife?
Explain the significance of this.

What sword threatens to sever your oneness with your
spouse?

God came to save individuals, not marriages. Helping a couple get along at the expense of either spouse's salvation is not God's plan. What guidance does this truth offer you?

What is the hope in this truth?

Now explain why God places neither family nor marriage first. Why does He insist that He be first and foremost?

- Telling people that what they are doing is wrong does not give them the power to stop doing it. The core problem of a fallen humanity is their basic nature, not their behavior.

Review the discussion of our "Fallen Nature" (pp. 63-65). What do you see about yourself as you look into this mirror provided by Scripture?

In Romans 7:7-25, Paul reflected on the nature of humankind and on his personal struggle to do the good he wanted to do and not do the evil he didn't want to do. In your marriage, what good do you want to do, but don't?

What evil do you *not* want to do, but do anyway?

- Problems in struggling marriages are due to the unre-solved personal and spiritual conflicts that keep couples from having a Christ-centered marriage. Simply changing our behavior will not resolve the essential problems. It is our responsibility to believe the truth and allow God to transform us.

What did you learn from the teaching on "A New Nature" (pp. 65-67)?

What inaccurate understanding did it clear up or what hope did it reinforce for you?

What will you do to put yourself in the position for God to change your heart?

Evaluate to what degree you are living your life in depen-dence on Him. What areas of your life have you not yet com-pletely surrendered to Him?

- Every child of God shares in His rich inheritance, has the power to live victoriously in Christ, and has authority over the evil one as long as he or she is strong in the Lord. Problems arise when we don't realize this truth.

Review the "Who I Am in Christ" statements on pages 67-68. Which truths do you struggle to believe? Make a list of them and memorize them. In fact, it would be beneficial to begin to memorize all of the verses in the list as a hedge against future times of doubt.

Imagine that you full-heartedly believed these truths at every moment, how would your life be different?

What would your confidence level be like?

How would your priorities be different?

What difference would believing these truths make in your marriage? Be specific.

What will you do to appropriate these truths and make them part of your way of thinking? Prayer, Bible study and Scripture memorization are good beginning steps.

- God views marriage in the context of sanctification, the process of conforming us to His image. When each of us makes our relationship with God first in our lives, then we can become the husbands and fathers or wives and mothers that He wants us to be.

  The greatest commandment is "'Love the Lord your God with all your heart and with all your soul and with all your mind. This is the first and greatest commandment. And the second is like it: "Love your neighbor as yourself." All the Law and the Prophets hang on these two commandments'" (Matthew 22:37-40).

What interferes with your ability to love God with your whole being?

What keeps you from loving your neighbor—especially your mate—as yourself?

How, if at all, is your service for God an enemy of your devotion to Him?

- Taking our cross (see Matthew 10:38) means that we willingly choose to totally identify with Christ, say no to sin and self-rule, and obediently follow His leading.

In what ways have you said no to sin and self-rule in your marriage this week?

In what area of your relationship with your spouse do you need to follow Christ's leading?

In 1 Timothy 4:8, Paul teaches "physical training is of some value, but godliness has value for all things, holding promise for both the present life and the life to come." Describe your current training program for godliness.

What improvements could, or will, you make?

What hope for yourself and for your marriage do you find in 2 Corinthians 5:17, "If anyone is in Christ, he is a new creation; the old has gone, the new has come!"?

- Understanding the truth that "the Spirit himself testifies with our spirit that we are God's children" (Romans 8:16) is critical because people cannot consistently behave in ways that are inconsistent with how they perceive themselves. The Holy Spirit is the inner testimony of our relationship to God.

It is not what we do that determines who we are; it is who we are that determines what we do. How does the fact that you are a child of God impact what you do, or how should it impact what you do?

Similarly, how we perceive others will have great impact on how we relate to them. How should the fact that your spouse is a child of God affect how you relate to him or her?

The world bases personal identity and worth on appearance, performance and/or social status. Marriage and children interfere with all three attributes. How has having a spouse and children affected your efforts to look good, perform well and/or maintain high social status?

Are you pursuing the world's standards and goals or God's?

How are your goals affecting your marriage?

QUESTIONS FOR FURTHER STUDY OR GROUP INTERACTION:

NOTES FROM GROUP INTERACTION OR PERSONAL COUNSELING:

Conforming to His Image

When we look to our marriages and families to find our sense of identity and worth, they become potential enemies. When we look to God to discover who we are and why we are here, then our marriages and families become the primary instruments He uses to conform us to His image.

- A married person should not take on the responsibility of changing his or her spouse's character. However, Scripture teaches that each person *is* responsible for the development of his or her own character and for meeting the needs of his or her spouse.

How would you describe your marriage in relation to the previous paragraph?

Apart from your spouse, write down your three greatest needs.

Write down your spouse's three greatest needs.

Compare your lists and discuss the following:

In what ways are these needs being met?

In what ways would you like your spouse to help meet your needs? Is this realistic?

- Both a husband and wife may feel so deprived of their own basic needs that they can't see beyond them. Being married does not resolve the core personal needs that can only be met in Christ.

  Before starting to work on your marriage, identify any core personal needs that you need to resolve in Christ. Then turn to Appendix A in *The Christ-Centered Marriage* and learn how to let Christ meet your needs and resolve your conflicts.

What core personal needs—which can only be met by Christ—does your mate still need to resolve? You may be able to talk about this. Whether or not you can discuss these needs with your spouse, pray that he or she will come to realize the need for Christ's touch and that God will begin to do a work of deliverance in his or her life.

- If we are free in Christ and living in the center of God's will, we will feel good about ourselves. There are, however, four personal and cultural misperceptions that run counter to this principle. These include a preoccupation with individual rights, trying to be another person's conscience, confusing judgment with discipline and not sharing personal needs with loved ones.

It's easier to demand our individual rights than to assume our personal responsibilities. Where is this true in your marriage?

In what ways have you *demanded* that your spouse respect you or submit to you?

Wives: In what specific ways do you submit to your husband as the Church submits to Christ (see Ephesians 5:22-33)?

Husbands: In what specific ways are you demonstrating a Christlike love for your wife (see Ephesians 5:22-33)?

- We cannot play the role of being another person's conscience. Only the Holy Spirit has the rightful role of being someone's conscience.

In what ways have you acted as your spouse's conscience?

What can you do to show your mate unconditional love and acceptance?

There is an important distinction between discipline and judgment. Discipline is related to a person's behavior, whereas judgment is related to a person's character. Attacks made on character cannot be resolved; however, confronting someone on the basis of behavior can resolve the situation.

Think about the last time (or last few times) you confronted your spouse. Did you address behavior or character?

What changes do you want to make in what and how you communicate?

Now think about how you respond to your spouse's words—consider both your attitude and your own words. What changes do you want to make in how you respond?

How do you share your needs with your spouse? Do you tend to share your needs appropriately with an "I" statement or do you tend to put your mate on the defensive with a "you" judgment?

What current need(s) do you want to share with your spouse? Stop for a moment and plan how you will tell your spouse about your needs. Also plan how you will respond the next time your spouse shares his or her needs.

- We must not run away from our marriage and family commitments and responsibilities because, among other reasons, God can use these relationships to conform us to Christ's image.

In your relationship with your spouse what situations or experiences has God used to develop more Christlike patience, kindness, love, prayerfulness, compassion, gentleness, forgiveness and other godly qualities in you? Be specific.

Think about how God has worked in your spouse's life since you have been married. In what specific way has your spouse become more Christlike? Let him or her know the growth you see.

Becoming more like Christ *is* the good that God wants to work in the life of each of His children (see Romans 8:28). What other good fruit (see Romans 5:3-5) has come from the trials and tribulations you and your mate have endured together?

If you are currently dealing with trials and tribulations at home, what can you change about yourself that might improve the situation?

Commit yourself to being the best possible wife and mother or husband and father God wants you to be, and believe that God will transform you in your marriage.

• God works through committed relationships, namely our spouses and children, to make us more Christlike because those that live with us can see right through us.

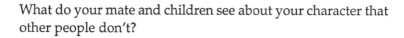

What do your mate and children see about your character that other people don't?

What do your mate and children see about your walk of faith that other people don't?

What does this say about the aspects of your character that you need to change?

Read Colossians 3:9-21 and ask God to help you put off the old self and put on the new self.

- Every Christian is a child of God. This is the core of our identities. However, we do not live with perfect people, therefore forgiving one another is the first step in loving others. Jesus said, "'A new command I give you: Love one another. As I have loved you, so you must love one another'" (John 13:34).

When we know who we are in Christ, we can be people who obey God's call to forgive. What bitterness or unresolved anger are you carrying?

Whom do you need to forgive? From whom do you need to ask forgiveness?

Forgiving one another is the first step in loving one another the way God loves, not because the object of love is lovable but because God, who dwells in us, is love.

When has God's grace enabled you to love your spouse or a child?

In what family situation today do you need God to help you love someone? Ask Him for the help you need to love your spouse and children.

What will you do today to follow in the footsteps of Christ (see 1 John 3:16-18) and make laying down your life for your spouse a reality?

The key to a godly character is letting the Word of Christ dwell in our hearts (Colossians 3:16). What are you doing to let God's Word dwell in your heart?

What could you do to make God's truth the solid foundation for your marriage and home?

QUESTIONS FOR FURTHER STUDY OR GROUP INTERACTION:

NOTES FROM GROUP INTERACTION OR PERSONAL COUNSELING:

Disappointment with Marriage

No one is perfect. Marriage partners let us down in big ways and small. How are we to handle them? How can the stumbling blocks of marriage and family life become stepping stones for God's glory and others' good?

- Disappointment can result in a stronger, more mature marriage when we respond in an honest and loving way. God calls us to purify our spirits by forgiving one another, reevaluating the situation and the way we confront our spouses.

How do you deal with disappointment in your marriage?

What wrong reactions and self-protective behaviors do you need to let go of?

What can you do to be quicker to forgive?

Why do certain things hurt as much as they do?

What can you do to improve communication?

What attitude can you readjust?

What is the most effective way for you to lovingly confront your spouse when you are disappointed?

David Augsburger describes the four stages of marriage as "The Dream of the 20s," "The Disillusionment of the 30s," "The Discovery of the 40s" and "The Depth of the 50s." Even if the ages don't correspond exactly for you, how well does this description fit your years of marriage? Be specific about what you've experienced in each stage.

The biggest disappointments of marriage sometimes hide the finest benefits. Years of living with his tempestuous wife taught Abraham Lincoln patience, tolerance, humor, forbearance and forgiveness. What benefits have come from the disappointments in your marriage?

- Anger, rebellion and manipulation are major causes of disappointment in marriage.

Anger can either foul up a marriage or protect it. When has your anger or your spouse's anger protected your marriage?

How is any anger that you're feeling now fouling up or threatening your marriage?

Review pages 94-98. How is destructive anger like a swamp? Describe the swamp you may find yourself in today.

The first paragraph of the section entitled "Anger" (pp. 94-95) describes when it is appropriate to be angry and when it is not. Think about times you have been angry. At what times have you been inappropriately angry? At what times have you expressed your anger appropriately?

Read the following Scriptures quoted in the section on anger and then comment on what the Bible teaches about anger and how you can apply the teaching to your life:

Proverbs 29:11

Ephesians 2:13-18

Ephesians 4:26,27

Ephesians 4:31,32

Ephesians 6:10-20

Colossians 3:19

James 1:19,20

- Rebellion is another source of disappointment in marriage, and rebellion can occur when submission is misunderstood.

What does the Bible mean by the instruction to submit and how is that different from how our culture interprets submission?

Why is biblical submission a win-win situation for both husband and wife?

In what areas of your relationship do you need to voluntarily yield your rights to your spouse in love? More simply, in what ways can you put the other person first? Be specific.

- The refusal to submit to God and your spouse can result in manipulation—another cause of disappointment in marriage. At the heart of manipulation is a refusal to trust God.

What lessons do the experiences of Isaac, Abimelech and Rebekah, and later, Rebekah, Jacob and Isaac (pp. 100-101) offer about the disappointment that results from manipulation?

Reread David Augsburger's "The Art of Manipulation" on pages 104-105. In what ways do you try to manipulate your spouse?

Marriage is built on respect, but we lose respect for one another when we base our respect on the other person's behavior. Since no one is perfect, it is only in Christ that you can learn to respect your mate's person and his or her position in your life. What reasons for respecting your spouse do you find in God's Word?

In His Son's death on the cross?

In your spouse's position in God's family?

What specific things can you do to show your mate that you respect him or her? Choose one specific action to do today.

- Think back on the disappointments you've experienced in life.

Where was God during those disappointments or difficult experiences?

God is as close as the air you breathe. What hope does this wonderful truth give you for your marriage?

For your parenting?

For your own spiritual growth?

Pray the "Clay Pot's Prayer" (pp. 106-107) aloud to your heavenly Father.

Read again the section entitled "Fork in the Road" (pp. 107-109). What danger lies in turning to non-Christian counselors and therapists for help in getting in touch with your deep feelings?

What does a biblical counselor offer that a non-Christian cannot?

Does the road you're on lead to self-sufficiency or Christ-sufficiency? Identify road markers to support your answer.

QUESTIONS FOR FURTHER STUDY OR GROUP INTERACTION:

NOTES FROM GROUP INTERACTION OR PERSONAL COUNSELING:

Created Male, Created Female

The differences between male and female extend far beyond physical characteristics. Men and women, for instance, hold within their souls different ways of seeing the world, different dialects for communicating, and different ways of coping with stress.

- The opening of the chapter gives us two pictures of the marriage relationship, one from nature and one from the Bible.

The two little birds give us a vivid image of teamwork by showing us...

> Efficiency through division of labor;
> Resting after failure;
> Working hard until success comes;
> Defending home and family;
> Providing resources hour after hour, day after day;
> Creating design and beauty;
> Furnishing shelter, protection and privacy;
> Preparing diligently for the future.

How is this kind of teamwork evident in your marriage? Give specific examples for each item.

On a separate sheet of paper, write an "I appreciate you" note to your spouse, touching on some or all of the eight lessons observed in the birds' teamwork. Include any other personal examples of teamwork as well.

Review the Bible's teachings about marriage in Genesis 2:18,20-24 and Ephesians 5:22-33.

Wife: What does your husband, the loving, sacrificing head of the family, do to show his love? Be specific.

Husband: What could you do to be more loving?

What sacrifices is God nudging you to make for your wife's sake and for the benefit of the marriage?

Husband: How is your wife a "suitable helper" to you?

How does she complement you? Be specific.

Wife: What could you do to be more helpful to your husband?

What effort is God calling you to make on your husband's behalf and for the sake of your marriage?

- Both men and women share the image of God and yet their differences extend far beyond their physical characteristics. Men and women vary in how they see and respond to the world.

Describe the difference between men's and women's viewpoints.

Discuss with your spouse the insights you gained from this discussion.

What one concept from this discussion would you like your spouse to especially notice about your gender?

Make a date to explain to your spouse why you value these differences.

What new behavior, attitude and response to your spouse will result from your new understanding of these hidden differences?

• Women and men have differing styles of communicating.

The following is a list of the differences between men's and women's communication styles. As you read them together try to think of specific examples from your own experiences that illustrate these differences.

Women share feelings.	Men share facts.
Women thrive on communication.	Men thrive on action.
Women desire verbal relationships.	Men desire companionship.
Concerning a difficulty or a crisis: Women express thoughts and emotions.	Men want to solve the problem.

How do these differing qualities make your marriage whole?

If your marriage were based *only* on facts and actions or *only* on feeling and relationship, what would you imagine your relationship to be like?

- Men and women vary in how they understand sexuality.

Describe the differences between men and women in their understanding of sexuality.

Husband: What kind of emotional feelings do you experience when you are having sex?

Wife: Explain why conversation, relaxation and tenderness increase your desire for sex.

Share your answers to the previous questions.

If you have never done so, share with one another those attitudes, actions or responses that increase your desire and pleasure during lovemaking.

- Men and women vary in the way they handle stress. Men will take time out to be alone, no matter who they may hurt in the process. Women will find time to share their feelings, whether or not their husbands will listen.

Husband: Explain to your wife how you handle stress. What is your "cave" (pp. 120-122)—recreation, sleep, work, TV?

How would you like to be supported by your wife during times of stress?

What will you do to reassure your wife the next time you're in your cave?

Wife: What is most difficult for you when your husband is in his cave?

Husband: How do you react (inwardly and outwardly) when your wife expresses her cascading emotions (see pp. 122-124)? Do you:

Distance yourself?   Feel helpless?   Want to understand?

Problem solve?   Run away?   Simply listen?

Wife: What can your husband do to create a sheltered beach for you where your waves can ebb and flow?

- The differences between women and men make up much of the magnetism that draws us together in marriage. We are to use our uniqueness to meet one another's needs, help each other and encourage each other. The better we understand our differences, the more we will appreciate each other's strengths.

What difference(s) first attracted you to your spouse?

What strengths do you especially appreciate in your spouse? This list may overlap your list of differences!

QUESTIONS FOR FURTHER STUDY OR GROUP INTERACTION:

NOTES FROM GROUP INTERACTION OR PERSONAL COUNSELING:

Resolving Conflicts

Many couples perceive their differences as weaknesses, rather than trying to understand and complement each other because of those differences. But God intended those differences to be the strength of your marriage.

- Marriages can potentially thrive on conflict if it is handled constructively. No husband and wife will see life from the same perspective, nor perfectly agree about how it should be lived.

Make a list of the differences in background, tastes, interests, etc. between you and your spouse.

How do these differences make your spouse your perfect mate?

Reread the first paragraph on page 127, describing how Neil and Joanne have influenced each other for the better over the years.

Give one example of how you and your mate have influenced one another for the better.

• A primary problem in marriages today is a lack of husbands providing spiritual leadership. Consequently the functional head in most homes is the wife. Being submissive to someone who will not lead is like being a passenger in a car with a driver who doesn't know where he's going and does not obey the rules of the road.

What is it like to be a passenger in a car...

When the driver doesn't know where he is going and will not stop to ask for directions?

When the driver does not obey the rules of the road?

When you know the driver is headed in the right direction?

When the driver safely obeys the rules of the road?

Husband: What insight does this analogy of driver and passenger give you into your wife's experiences as your mate?

Wife: What kind of marriage "passenger" are you being? Circle one.

Nagger   Bossy   Complainer   Companion

- Being the head of a home is not a right to be demanded; it is an awesome responsibility. Husbands will have to stand before God someday and give account for what has been entrusted to them.

Husband: What have you done as the head of your household to ensure that Christ is the center of your life, your marriage and your family?

What are you intentionally doing to guide your wife and children into being who God created them to be? What, if anything, are you or others doing that hinders them from this goal?

Wife: What has your husband done to contribute to your family's well-being in terms of protection, provision and as a source of spiritual strength?

In what ways is your husband helping you to be who God created you to be?

In what ways do you need to be more supportive of your husband's efforts to be the spiritual leader of your family?

Husband and wife: Read Ephesians 5:22-33 and Philippians 2:1-8. What qualities did Jesus have that equipped Him to be the head of the Church?

Read Matthew 20:25-28. How is being the head of the household like being a servant?

- Refusing to be submissive simply because we don't like our less-than-perfect authorities is rebellion. Trusting God to work in our lives through less-than-perfect government officials, employers, husbands and parents requires great faith.

In what ways have you "taken things into your own hands" by not properly submitting to those in authority over you? Do you always have to have your own way or, on the other extreme, are you overly passive when you should take leadership?

How self-aware are you when it comes to rebelling against God? Do you know when you have rebelled against God in your heart or in your actions? How do you know?

Who *functions* as the leader in your household? What are the qualities of a godly leader?

Husband: Have you rebelled against God by not loving your wife?

Wife: Have you rebelled against God by not respecting your husband?

Husband: Have you made yourself worthy of respect?

Are you temperate, self-controlled and sound in faith, in love and in endurance?

Are you a person of integrity?

What character trait in you needs the most improvement?

Wife: Are you reverent, self-controlled, kind? Do you submit to your husband? Why or why not?

What character trait in you needs the most improvement?

It is not hard for a woman to be subject to a man of character who is in subjection to God. Does this describe your marriage or do you need to make adjustments?

- Iron does indeed sharpen iron, but not without a lot of heat, smoke and sparks. Conflict is inevitable in marriage and in any meaningful relationship. Without conflicts, relationships are merely superficial, unconstructive and stale. With conflicts, relationships grow and mature, mutual understanding occurs and intimacy deepens. However, how you and your spouse handle conflict is vital to making conflict work for your marriage rather than against your marriage.

  Referring to Diagram 7.1 "Conflict Styles" on page 133, answer the following questions:

1. Think about your parents' conflict styles. How did their conflict styles affect the way you think about conflict?

2. Which conflict style describes the way you handle conflict?

3. Which parent are you most like?

4. How well did you relate to this parent growing up? How well did you relate to your other parent?

5. Which conflict style best describes your spouse's way of handling conflict?

6. How does knowing your conflict styles change the way you will deal with conflict with your spouse?

No single right way to approach every conflict exists, but each style has its strengths and weaknesses. Knowing your style will allow you and your spouse to improve your way of handling conflict so that both of you will come away with a deeper sense of intimacy with one another and a deeper commitment to the solution. As you focus in unity upon the solution, your marriage will grow stronger and you will be more secure in your marriage. However, taken to an extreme, any conflict style can be counterproductive. The most insecure are those who routinely withdraw, manipulate or strive to win.

Think about the last several conflicts that you have had with your spouse. Were there personal attacks made against you? Were you the instigator of personal attacks? Or were you both able to keep your discussions confined to the issues?

Did you understand fully your spouse's point of view? Did you feel understood to your satisfaction? What is it like to feel misunderstood?

How do you know when your spouse understands your point of view?

What will you do to let your spouse know that you do understand fully?

Having diverse perspectives does not mean that your marriage is flawed, but rather, your marriage is strengthened by your differences. Alone, one does not necessarily know the best solution to a problem, but diversity opens opportunities to gain vision for new options that would otherwise never have been discovered.

Review the "Destructive when..." and "Constructive when..." lists on pages 135-136 and then answer the following questions:

What is the value of having differing opinions and perspectives?

Do you view conflict as a win-lose problem or do you strive for a win-win solution?

In all honesty, would you rather have your own way or will you sacrifice your way in favor of doing things God's way?

Do you give your spouse the benefit of the doubt?

Is your spouse sincerely concerned for the marriage or just argumentative and pushy?

Do you believe that by earnestly listening to your spouse's perspective that you will come to an agreement that is even better than any one individual's suggestions or do you have to get your own point of view across no matter what?

- Constructive conflict resolution results in unity and a high level of trust. Sharing is open and honest, and it is not necessary to agree with everything everyone else says. What is important is that all parties have an equal opportunity to express their views and share their feelings.

  We learned to communicate from our parents. Diagram 7.2 on page 137 presents different styles of communication. According to the diagram:

1. Which communication style typified your father and how has that affected you?

2. Which communication style typified your mother and how has that affected you?

3. Which communication style best describes your style?

4. Which parent are you most like?

5. How well did you relate to this parent as you were growing up?

6. Which communication style best describes your spouse's
   style?

7. How does knowing yours and your spouse's different
   communication styles affect your relationship?

How does your regard for relationships, whether it is high or
low, affect your ability to communicate?

What changes in your communication style would improve
conflict resolution in your marriage?

What is the first step you will take toward making that change?

Respond to the 20 agree/disagree statements about communication on pages 138-139 and compare your answers with your mate's. What does this exercise reveal about communication in your marriage?

Are the two of you on the same wavelength or have you discovered areas that need further discussion and mutual understanding? Set a time to discuss any areas of serious disagreement.

QUESTIONS FOR FURTHER STUDY OR GROUP INTERACTION:

NOTES FROM GROUP INTERACTION OR PERSONAL COUNSELING:

Love Language

One of the finest skills anyone can master is love language. In fact, learning to speak your spouse's love language just might revolutionize your marriage.

- In his book *The Five Love Languages*, Gary Chapman identifies the languages as gifts, service, time, touch and words.

What love language(s) do you prefer? Let your spouse know!

What love language(s) does your mate prefer?

In what ways have you been communicating love in your love language(s) rather than in your mate's?

• Let's take a quick inventory of your multilingualism! Sometimes when we are showing our spouse love, he or she doesn't receive our love because we are communicating in our own love language rather than in our spouse's love language—and that works both ways.

   As you review the discussion of each love language, note the examples given and then answer the following questions as specifically as you can.

Gifts: What gifts do you give your spouse?

What gifts would your spouse enjoy receiving from you?

Service: What do you do to serve your mate and show your love?

What other service would make your spouse feel loved?

Time: Men often focus on *doing* and women on *feeling* when they consider spending time together. To what degree are these gender stereotypes true in your marriage?

What kind of time do you give your spouse as a way of communicating your love?

What way of spending time would make your spouse feel even more loved?

Touch: What kinds of touch does your spouse like, and when?

What kind of touch would your spouse like to experience?

Words: "I love you" and specific compliments about character, ability and intimacy build up a marriage. What words do you offer your mate?

How often do you say them?

What words would your mate like to hear for the first time—or hear more often?

- Now consider the love language(s) your spouse is speaking to you and which ones you hear more clearly.

Gifts: What gifts does your spouse give you?

What gifts would you like to receive from your spouse?

Service: What does your mate do to serve you?

What other acts of service would make you feel loved?

Time: What kind of time does your spouse give you?

What kind of time would make you feel even more loved?

Touch: What kind of touch do you like, and when?

What kind of touch would you like to experience?

Words: What words does your mate use to build you up?

What words would you like your mate to use—or use more often?

- Now, gently and sensitively, talk with your spouse about your answers to these questions regarding love language(s). This step is crucial because, after all, neither of you is a mind reader.

As a result of your conversation, what new ways of saying "I love you" can you try? List at least five ways.

Which form of "I love you" will you use this week?

- Now expand your focus from your spouse to your children or other close family members or friends.

List their names below and note their emotional love languages next to them. If you aren't sure, find out. Next to each person's name and language, jot down a few things you can do to say "I love you" in the language they prefer—and do one of them this week.

Name	Language	What I can do to say "I love you"
_____	_____	_____
		_____
_____	_____	_____
		_____
_____	_____	_____
		_____
_____	_____	_____
		_____
_____	_____	_____
		_____
_____	_____	_____

- Most of us tend to give love in the ways we most want to receive love. If we are blind to how we're different from our family and friends, people will not receive our love as fully as they would if it came in their own preferred love language.

What changes in the way you communicate your love to others are you going to make? Give specifics in each category.

Gifts:

Service:

Time:

Touch:

Words:

QUESTIONS FOR FURTHER STUDY OR GROUP INTERACTION:

NOTES FROM GROUP INTERACTION OR PERSONAL COUNSELING:

The Lust for Money

Remember the peanut vendor? Like him, you and I are turning down a partnership with the Lord of unlimited riches when we don't commit all of our finances to God.

* God puts the longing for security in our hearts, but real security is found only by seeking first His kingdom (see Matthew 6:25-34), His rule and His government.

When have you experienced insecurity based on money? Be specific.

When have you experienced most tangibly the rock-solid security of God?

Jesus calls us to seek God's kingdom first. Dallas Willard describes the Kingdom as "the effective range of God's will." What aspects of your life—your own kingdom—are not yet under God's daily control?

What about your life does not conform to His will? Consider your attitude, motivations, worship life, thought life, marriage, family and—yes—finances.

Does your use of money fall into God's jurisdiction or yours? Support your answer with some specific evidence from your life.

Review the five biblical truths listed under "Craving Money" (p. 165). What do you see about yourself in this image?

Next, take a few moments to make a fearless moral inventory. As you read through the Bible passages listed on page 165, ask yourself *Who do I really serve between Sundays? Is it the God who revealed Himself in Jesus Christ, or is it money? Does my money help me serve God or do I expect God to help me make more money?* Support your answers with specific examples of your attitudes and behaviors.

- Money has a good side and a bad side. On the good side money provides for our daily needs, supports God's work and enables us to enjoy a few luxuries in life. The bad side is that the love of money also destroys compassion, self-sacrifice and the intensity of our love for God.

How is money currently contributing to the level of peace or pain in your marriage? Are you seeing God's provision and enjoying the peace of resting in Him, or are you finding that the love of money is indeed destroying your compassion, self-sacrifice and love for God in your marriage?

What can and will you do to minimize the pain and destruction money is causing?

- Pain caused by the love of money can often be reduced by obeying God's command to tithe, an obedience illustrated by the story "The Ten Apples" (p. 166).

When did you first hear about the biblical principle of tithing?

How did you react?

What impact did learning about tithing have on your life?

What does your current checkbook register reflect about your love for God? Are you giving Him that one red apple, that 10 percent of your income, or are you giving Him only the core—the leftovers?

If God is getting only an apple core, what is keeping you from seeking God's will about tithes and offerings?

Ask God to transform you in the area of tithing as only God can do.

Listed below are five guidelines for a believer in our material-istic society. Add a specific instruction or two after each item to give you direction in putting these guidelines into practice.

1. Admit that God is the owner of everything, including your money.

   _____

2. Learn contentment, the kind that comes with godliness.

   _____

3. Find delight in simple pleasures.

   _____

4. Become a wise steward of all the resources God gives, including your finances.

   _____

5. Give more; live on less.

   _____

• Believing God's truth precedes living Christ's way. To put it simply, we must believe God's truth about money before we will change our spending habits. We must honor God with our finances before we can expect Him to honor us with inner contentment.

Is money a point of contention in your marriage? What deci-sions are most difficult?

What issues recur in your discussions about finances?

Why can the truth that God owns everything help loosen our hold on money and defuse discussions of money?

What specific financial decisions that you currently or regularly face can this truth clarify and simplify?

- God does indeed own everything. Genuine belief in this truth will lead us to...

  Acknowledge that all money and material things in our care belong to God.

  Pursue good management of the Lord's money and resources.

  Consult the Lord and seek wise counsel in financial decisions.

  Pray, "Give us today our daily bread."

  Rejoice in knowing that God provides and blesses.

  Learn contentment when God withdraws financial resources and teaches trust.

  Actually act like God is in charge of our money!

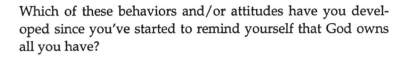

Which of these behaviors and/or attitudes have you developed since you've started to remind yourself that God owns all you have?

Which behavior and/or attitude do you want to work on next?

What will you do to reach that goal?

Again, are you tithing—or are you merely tipping? What painful consequences have you suffered as a result of just tipping, or what pleasurable blessings have you received since you started tithing?

- Our financial goal in marriage is not to become rich, but to become content in Christ. Contentment comes from security in Christ and from good stewardship of the money God gives us. Consider more closely the following steps toward contentment:

1. Sign it all over to God.

   What will you do to rivet God's ownership in your minds? Join with your spouse and write a quitclaim deed, make a prayer of commitment, and/or change your pronouns from "our" and "mine" to "the."

2. Practice gratitude.

   Make a list of all that God has provided for you and every day thank Him for these blessings, producing a habit of gratitude.

3. Resolve differences.

   Make a list of your needs—and a list of your wants. Compare your lists to your spouse's lists and be open to his or her input regarding your needs and wants. Also, determine together what percentage of your income you will give to the Lord's work and what percentage you will save—and start giving and saving now!

4. Manage finances wisely.

   Write out a budget starting with the entry for tithing followed closely by the entry for saving.

5. Reduce debt.

   Does your budget enable you to reduce the debt you're carrying? If not, revise your budget and decide which of the other ten guidelines for debt reduction you will follow (see number 5, pages 172-173).

6. Give generously.

What, if anything, keeps you from giving generously?

Which of the following three biblical principles will you act on today?
- ❑ Give before you can afford it.
- ❑ Give beyond your ability.
- ❑ Give yourself first to the Lord.

7. Invest wisely.

Why are you saving?

What are your goals?

What are you doing to ensure that you are investing God's money wisely?

- In a culture devoted to greed and built upon the false god of money, every Christian and every godly family needs a code of financial ethics. After all, money used wisely for God's glory helps build a happy marriage. Money mis-used foolishly for personal gain helps create an unhappy marriage.

Review and discuss together the 12 Bible-based principles for financial ethics outlined here (see pages 174-175 for scriptural support).

1. Avoid greed and be honest.
2. Show God's love with the money He entrusts to you.
3. Pay debts promptly and seek to stay out of debt.
4. Save for future difficulties.
5. Avoid risky investments.
6. Use investment money for God's glory.
7. Live by the highest standards for financial integrity in your family, church and work.
8. Neither oppress the poor nor bribe the rich.
9. Make restitution for any wrongs committed against the person or property of another.
10. Do not use the courts for lawsuits against other believers or engage in any unethical legal proceedings designed to gain unjust money.
11. Work faithfully and diligently for your income.
12. Balance work and rest.

Put a star by the principles which are already in place in your financial dealings.

Put an arrow by those items you need to act on and write down the first specific step you'll take toward those goals.

Now close in prayer, asking God to transform your heart so that you can know the freedom and joy that come with living out the truth that God owns everything. Ask Him, too, to help you submit to the rule of King Jesus over both your marriage and your money.

QUESTIONS FOR FURTHER STUDY OR GROUP INTERACTION:

NOTES FROM GROUP INTERACTION OR PERSONAL COUNSELING:

Sexual Freedom

Sexual bondage destroys many marriages, and the origin of the problem can usually be traced to lust or to pornography, promiscuity, incest or rape before marriage. Getting married will not resolve it. Only Christ can.

- Wouldn't it be great if we all had perfect parents who taught us the truth about love and sex? Such is not the case.

Consider the question, Does a wife have to do whatever her husband wants her to do in bed? Discuss with your spouse the biblical guidelines presented on pages 178-179. With what points do you agree or disagree? Why?

What did you learn about love and sex from your parents? What picture of sexuality did they give you? Consider what they didn't say as well as what they did say.

How has your parents' model affected your ability to be affectionate, physically demonstrative and/or comfortable with your own sexuality?

What lessons about and attitudes toward sexuality has your spouse brought into your marriage?

How have these ideas and attitudes impacted your relationship?

• Having looked at what our parents taught us about sexuality, let's see what the life of King David teaches about sexuality, specifically temptation, sin and its consequences.

When faced with sexual temptation, what way of escape did David choose to ignore (see 2 Samuel 11:1-5)?

Reread the story of the man who went to the store to buy milk for his wife (page 181-182). What ways of escape did he ignore? How did he rationalize his behavior?

Why do we human beings ignore the ways of escape—the paths of mercy—that God provides when we are tempted by sin?

What path of mercy is described in 2 Corinthians 10:3-5?

What exactly does a believer need to do to walk that path specifically in regard to sexual temptation?

What chain of events followed David's adulterous act (see 2 Samuel 11:4-17)?

Who also suffered as a result of David's sin (see 2 Samuel 11:17,26; 12:15-19)?

What judgment from God did David experience?

What do your answers to the questions about David's sin and its consequences reveal about God's perspective on sexual immorality?

- Sexual sin often leads the guilty party to live a dual life. Such was the case for David.

What does Matthew 10:26 say about such a dual life?

What does Psalm 32:1-5 reveal about the internal, emotional turmoil following David's sin?

What do Psalm 32 and the anecdotes in "A Dual Life" (see pages 183-184) suggest about the way out of sexual sin?

- God also reveals His perspective on sexuality through the writings of the apostle Paul in 1 Corinthians 6:19,20.

What does it mean to you personally that your body is "a temple of the Holy Spirit" (v. 19)?

How does this truth impact your day-to-day living (your diet, dress, sleep, exercise and your sexual activities)?

What does it mean to you that your spouse's body is a temple of the Holy Spirit?

What does it mean for your sexual relationship?

The apostle Paul taught that we are alive in Christ, "Therefore do not let sin reign in your mortal body so that you obey its evil desires" (Romans 6:12). Where, if at all, is sin reigning in your body? What will you do to dethrone it?

Consider the accounts of Christian women being sexually involved with immoral men. What did these incidents illustrate about sexual bonding and about the loss of freedom which comes when we use our bodies as instruments of unrighteousness?

What do you do as a way of offering your body to God (see Romans 6:13)? Be specific.

What do you do to stand strong against any temptation to use your body as an instrument of wickedness? Be specific.

• Someone who has had "unholy" sex has difficulty enjoying "holy" sex. Promiscuity before marriage leads to a lack of fulfillment after marriage. When the relationships we have with God and with our spouse are the two most important in our lives, sex becomes the most intimate and vulnerable means of expressing love.

How has unholy sex or promiscuity impacted your marriage?

What has your study of God's Word in this chapter reminded you about His plan for sexuality?

Spend some time alone with God. Ask Him to reveal every sexual use of your body as an instrument of unrighteousness. Repent of those actions and then receive His forgiveness and the freedom He offers, for "if we confess our sins, he is faithful and just and will forgive us our sins and purify us from all unrighteousness" (1 John 1:9).

Now, in prayer, commit your body to God as a living sacrifice, reserving the sexual use of your body solely for your spouse.

QUESTIONS FOR FURTHER STUDY OR GROUP INTERACTION:

NOTES FROM GROUP INTERACTION OR PERSONAL COUNSELING:

The Snakebite of Adultery

Human beings were created to live in relationship with God and with each other. This capacity to love and be loved is part of the image of God, and it is stamped within our sexuality. At its best, our sexuality reflects the very nature of God.

- Sex was God's idea, and therefore good in its original context. However, just as every other aspect of our lives, our sexuality is corrupted by our sin nature. The Bible warns us to cast off any foul cravings and deceitful desires that we might have in order to preserve the goodness of our sexuality and to make it holy unto God. However, we cannot put off the temptations of the flesh by our own effort; we need to rely on the grace of God, the work of Christ and the ministry of the Holy Spirit for our total transformation.

Think about the times you've had unholy thoughts and desires. How did you know that they were unholy?

Are you able to distinguish between what is holy and what is unholy? How do you make that distinction?

As a Christian, how do you respond to your unholy thoughts and desires? What do you do about them?

- Romans 12:2 says, "Do not conform any longer to the pattern of this world, but be transformed by the renewing of your mind. Then you will be able to test and approve what God's will is—His good, pleasing and perfect will."

When it comes to sin, why is the mind so important?

In what ways does your mind need to be renewed?

According to Romans 12:2, how can you know the perfect will of God?

How does His will compare to your will?

Read Titus 3:3. How has Christ helped you work through your harmful desires?

What is the evidence that you have had a former way of life but are now abiding in Christ?

- No one abandons a perfect wife or a perfect husband for someone else. The problem is that no one is perfect! Before we get to the serious problem of adultery, knowing that "there but for the grace of God go I," let's laugh a little at our imperfections.

Read again the "The Perfect Wife" and "The Perfect Husband" on pages 198-200.

Are your expectations of your spouse realistic? Identify the areas where you have too many expectations of your spouse.

Do you have any unrealistic expectations of yourself? What are they?

Discuss these insights with your spouse and come to an agreement about how you plan to reduce unrealistic expectations.

- Perfection is an impossible goal that often leads to depression. The only successful method for creating an ideal spouse is to become one yourself! However, only in Christ is anyone perfect.

Return to the descriptions of the perfect wife and perfect husband (pp. 198-200). Choose one trait you as a husband or wife would like to improve in yourself.

What specific step will you take in reaching your goal?

- Each of us can and should take responsibility for maintaining our own freedom and sexual purity in Christ. Each can take steps toward obedience, love, faith and maturity. But what about our spouses? No one can live the Christian life for another, not even the closest people in our lives. What can caring spouses do to avoid having their marriages fall on the rocks of adultery?

Meeting your spouse's felt needs is one of the best ways to show love. Willard Harley, Jr. describes this as making deposits in our spouse's love bank. Read the following list of urgent needs of husbands and wives. Then both husband and wife rank them in order of personal preference.

Husband	Felt Needs	Wife
_____	Affection	_____
_____	Sexual fulfillment	_____
_____	Conversation	_____
_____	Recreational companionship	_____
_____	Honesty and openness	_____
_____	An attractive mate	_____
_____	Financial support	_____
_____	Domestic support	_____
_____	Family commitment	_____
_____	Admiration	_____

Copy your spouse's ranking of his or her felt needs and then study them. What does your spouse's list teach you about how to better meet his or her needs?

- It is not by accident that the Bible calls Satan a serpent. He is more venomous than a rattlesnake because his poison destroys whole families. When it comes to sin, we sometimes suffer from deadly snakebites but ignore the snakes.

  Remember the image of Janyce flying into action to kill the rattlesnake? She ran to the garden, grabbed the shovel and raced back to the truck. After three swift blows, she killed the snake and buried its head. We need to follow her example. Like Janyce, when we first become aware of enticement toward adultery and the demonic snake behind it, we need to run for our spiritual weapons.

God's armor: Read Ephesians 6 and take an inventory of your armor. Which pieces need improvement?

What do you need to do to be able to use them in battle?

Powerful prayers: Evaluate your prayer life:

Do you pray regularly?

Do you pray regularly about your marriage?

    With your spouse?

    For protection against temptation?

    For the strength to stay faithful?

What steps will you take to improve your personal prayer life?

What steps will you take to improve your prayer life with your spouse?

Biblical counsel: Who can you go to with personal matters and receive a biblical perspective and godly advice?

What will you do to begin building those kinds of relationships if you don't currently have such a support?

Instant obedience: Why is *instant* obedience so crucial?

Why are we human beings often so sluggish in obeying God?

What can you do to counter that tendency?

Extra precautions: Consider your life and any source of sexual temptation. What precautions do or will you take so you are not led into temptation?

Pride goes before a fall! Evaluate your (false) sense of security when it comes to affairs. Do you believe you and your spouse are immune to adultery? If so, are either of you denying that you are being tempted? The greater the denial, the easier the deception, so deal with that snake openly!

How, if at all, is Satan distracting you from your marriage with sexual temptation?

What is your weakest area?

What unmet longings are you dealing with?

What unmet longings does your spouse feel? (If you don't know, ask!)

What can you do to offer greater intimacy, affection, companionship, understanding, communication, admiration, pleasure and respect? Be specific.

- Unmet longings in a marriage take their toll. The deceiver moves in on unmet longings, attacks the weakest point and produces diminishing respect. Thoughts such as the following are red flags:

  I'm depressed all the time. I'm so tired of being unhappy.
  I hate this marriage. I don't want to go on like this. Am I going to spend the rest of my life this way?
  It just isn't fair [and all the details why].
  Look at him (or her)! No way can I respect someone like that.
  I just don't want to be married anymore.

What red flags, if any, are calling you to prayer right now? Confess those thoughts to God and ask Him to give you new energy and hope for your marriage.

When diminishing respect connects with increasing expectations, the danger intensifies. Are any of your words and attitudes reflected here?

> "I'm putting more into this marriage than I'm
>   getting out of it."
> "I'm tired of living with my nose to the grind-
>   stone. When are you going to get a raise?
>   When will you stop squandering our money?"
> "You always...!"
> "You never...!"
> "Why don't you...?"

If any of these words could be yours, what specific steps will you take to replace them with words that will strengthen your marriage?

* Adultery develops in three stages—conversation, friendship and belonging.

What did the mythical couple who progressed through these three stages teach you (see pages 205-208)?

What did you learn from Judy and Peter? What hope did you find in their story?

If you are involved in an adulterous affair, it's past time for you to break it off. Three steps need to be taken to end the adulterous affair and recover from its effects:

1. Amputate immediately;
2. Find someone to hold you accountable;
3. Acknowledge the need to grieve and do so.

Time, effort and quite possibly some godly counsel will be needed. It will take everything you've got to rebuild what has been destroyed.

If you are having an affair or if you are simply having tender talk with a person of the opposite sex outside of the marriage, but not inside your marriage, read pages 211-214.

- Whether or not adultery is an issue, there is hope for your marriage:

    In the Cross where Jesus died for you and your snakebites;
    In the empty tomb from which Jesus rose to give you and your family hope and a future;
    In the throne of God where Jesus reigns to crush the head of the serpent and repel the snakes that threaten you.

QUESTIONS FOR FURTHER STUDY OR GROUP
INTERACTION:

NOTES FROM GROUP INTERACTION OR
PERSONAL COUNSELING:

Forgive Seventy Times Seven

It is essential that marriage partners resolve problems—far easier said than done. Our society teaches us many ways to cope with conflict, but forgiving is not one of them. Run, fight, quit, blame, accuse, give up, get depressed—these are all common ways people cope.

- In His written Word, God speaks clearly on the issue of forgiveness. His plan teaches the skill of heartfelt forgiveness and the practice of loving confrontation to resolve relationship problems.

Review the six Bible passages that open the chapter (pp. 215-216). Which passage is especially challenging to you? Why?

How did you react to the story of forgiveness told by the woman who wrote to "Dear Abby"?

Considering your own heart attitude, what makes it hard for you to forgive your spouse?

Refusing to forgive causes us trouble and defiles our spirits. When have you seen bitterness pollute a person?

Read Matthew 6:14,15. How does unforgiveness affect your relationship with God?

Read Matthew 18:21-35. Refusing to forgive means that God will not forgive us. It also means that we will be tormented (vv. 34,35). What torment are you currently experiencing because of a lack of forgiveness? (Physiological problems, depression, restlessness, inner turmoil and dissatisfaction are some common symptoms.)

According to Matthew 6:14; Mark 11:25; 2 Corinthians 2:10,11; Colossians 3:13 and Hebrews 12:15, what are some of the benefits of forgiving others?

Read Luke 23:32-34. How did Jesus handle forgiveness?

What was His motive for forgiving?

Who was He focused on while He was being sinned against?

- As God's people, we need to clearly understand forgiveness, obey His command to forgive (see Colossians 3:13) and recognize Him as the source of the power to forgive.

How do you define forgiveness?

Check off which of the following myths about forgiveness you have bought into:

❑   It is essential to feel good about the person who hurt you before you forgive him or her.

❑   Forgiving means rolling over and playing dead, acting like the wrong didn't happen.

❑   Forgiveness is excusing the sin.

❑   Forgiveness is justifying the sinner.

❑   Forgiveness is forgetting.

❑   Forgiveness puts a stamp of approval on the wrong deed.

❑   Forgiveness automatically rebuilds trust.

❑   Forgiveness makes you like the one who hurt you.

Counter each myth you've bought into by saying aloud or, on a separate sheet of paper, writing out each statement in the negative. For example, "Forgiveness does not mean rolling over and playing dead, acting like the wrong didn't happen."

•   To forgive is to take our hurts and painful memories to God and leave them at the Cross. It is also an agreement to live with any unavoidable consequences.

In light of this definition, when have you forgiven someone? What happened to your pain?

Although God commands us to forgive, why do we sometimes refuse to do so?

In the following passages, what do you learn from Jesus—our crucified and risen Savior—about forgiveness and love?

Luke 23:33,34 _____

John 3:16 _____

Romans 5:8 _____

1 John 3:16 _____

Read the poem on page 223. What is God saying to you through this description of how Jesus has forgiven and continues to forgive you?

What area is a stumbling block to forgiveness for you?

How have you played the martyr role? Or do you have a tendency to settle the score first?

Reread the poem through the eyes of forgiveness. What gives you the ability and strength to forgive?

How do you benefit from forgiving those who have wronged you?

Review the 10 steps to forgiveness on pages 224-226. Ask God to bring to mind the names or faces of every person you need to forgive. Think of one offense at a time. On a piece of paper answer the following questions:

Who sinned against you?

What is the offense?

There are consequences to sin. Some are avoidable, others are not. What were the *unavoidable* consequences?

In what ways did you fail to take responsibility for those consequences that could be avoided?

Now pray. Begin by asking Jesus to bring to mind the names or faces of the people you need to forgive. Then pray this simple prayer for each person:

> Lord, I forgive (name) for (specifically identify all offenses and painful memories or feelings).

Agree to live with any consequences God does not remove and know that He will help you survive and thrive once you've removed the bitter seed of unforgiveness.

NOTE: When you have completed your time of prayer, tear up and throw away your list of grievances.

Now review the following "What You Do Not Have to Do" statements:
1. You do not have to feel good about the person who hurt you either before or after you forgive.
2. You do not have to tell the other person about your resentful feelings unless Scripture or the Holy Spirit tells you to.
3. You don't have to wait until you are ready to forgive. You can obey God's Word right now.

What freedom does the preceding list offer you?

- Unless you are in the earliest stages of your marriage, you are sure to have some painful memories. One of the best ways to deal with these hurtful times with one another, or with others, is to forgive.

  Set aside a day for you and your spouse to work through Step Five of "Steps to Setting Your Marriage Free" (pp. 265-270).

QUESTIONS FOR FURTHER STUDY OR GROUP INTERACTION:

NOTES FROM GROUP INTERACTION OR PERSONAL COUNSELING:

When Only One Will Try

Most troubled marriages are evidenced by only one spouse willing to work on improving the relationship. The good news is that most of the spiritual bondage in the marriage can be broken by one Christian spouse.

- Before you work through this chapter, complete the individual Steps to Freedom in Christ in Appendix A of *The Christ-Centered Marriage* if you have not already done so. You should also work through the "Finding Personal Freedom in Your Marriage" steps which are available from Freedom in Christ Ministries, 491 E. Lambert Road, La Habra, CA 90631 (562) 691-9128.

What first step toward the freedom available in Christ will you take this week?

- You can't improve your marriage by trying to change what you do without allowing Christ to change who you are. Doing, *without being,* simply does not work.

What is the difference between *doing* and *being*?

- Neglecting Christ's good news that we can become free in our innermost beings—more whole and healthy than we ever dreamed possible—leads too many people to opt for divorce when the road gets rough.

What did you learn from the studies about children of divorce?

How closely have you come in contact with divorce? What impact did it have on you?

Do you consider divorce an option for yourself? Why or why not?

- Moving a marriage from the brink of divorce to freedom in Christ is never easy. It takes more than trying harder and developing better communication skills. It takes sacrifice, dedication and commitment. It takes adjusting your life to God's ways and believing and living out His truth.

What hope do you find in Lance and Wendy's story (pp. 235-236)?

What hope do Psalm 16:1; 69:29; and 147:3 give you for living with the pain and to tolerate the spouse who keeps hurting you?

- Pray and ask God to show you a believer of the same gender that you can turn to who will pray with you and believe in God's healing power for you while you work through the steps. Contact that person this week to see if he or she can support you with regular meetings and faithful prayers. If you are not sure who to turn to, contact your local church for assistance.

     When you're living with the pain of a difficult marriage, prayer should also be accompanied by living out the following principles:

> I will let you be responsible, and I will not know-
>   ingly contribute to your being irresponsible.
> I will not try to force you to be responsible by
>   nagging, condemning, scolding or demora-
>   lizing.
> I will not knowingly let you be irresponsible by
>   removing the consequences when you do what
>   is wrong.
> I will stand by you, care for you, cry with you; but
>   I will not bail you out time after time after time.
> I will not personally judge you, pretending I am
>   your judge instead of God.

Neither will I personally provide a shelter for your sin, pretending I am your savior instead of Christ.

I will love you, accept you, forgive you and give you a fresh start whenever you ask for it.

Choose at least one of these principles that you need to demonstrate in your relationship with your spouse this week. How do you intend to live out this principle?

Note: When the principle you chose has become a habit, choose another one to develop.

From the example of Jesus' treatment of Judas, what do you learn about how to treat someone who keeps hurting you?

- Your success in living out these principles is not dependent upon your spouse's behavior, attitude or response. The next time you see your spouse, remind yourself of these principles and live by them regardless of your spouse's actions. There will be times when you experience increased pain before things get better.

How will you garner strength during these difficult times?

- God provides all that we need when life is hard, when pain is ever-present or when our marriages are seemingly hopeless. So now our focus shifts from being or becoming the kind of person who can save or improve a marriage to one who is doing something about it. Having spent time making sure we are connected to Christ, we can now rely on Him as we work on our marriages.

  Wisdom is the bridge between being and doing. Wisdom takes who we are and who God is, and applies that knowledge to a real-life situation. Wisdom takes God's truth and puts it to work in our marriage.

What does James 1:2-7 teach us about the resulting benefits of trial and suffering?

According to James, what is God's response to those who ask for wisdom?

All who have received Christ and live in Him are united with His creativity. Ask the Holy Spirit to help you be creative—to give you a new idea that will work in your marriage, the right words just when you need them, a thought which proves helpful to your spouse or an appreciative way of showing your love. Expect Him to work His creative power through you—and thank Him when He does!

- Remember Janice and Ted (pp. 241-243)? Each night Ted would come home for dinner and then spend the night at his girlfriend's house, completely disregarding his marriage commitment to Janice. But Janice was willing and eager to fight for her marriage and was consequently challenged to treat her husband just as she would treat Jesus even though her husband was not acting Christlike.

What happened when Janice began treating Ted as she would have treated Jesus?

Like Janice, make a plan to *love* and *serve* your spouse. For one week treat your spouse just as you would treat Jesus. Describe specifically what the activities and interactions of a typical day will look like as you adopt this approach. You may want to review "Love Language" (Chapter 8, pp. 141-157) as you plan your strategy. Let this be your game plan and, with prayer, get started now.

One of the best ways to strengthen a marriage is to compile a list of excuses your spouse makes to justify his or her actions. As you compile your list, begin to think of practical actions you can take to remove every cause for his or her excuse.

Surprisingly, the marriage partner who is not trying usually is neither pleased nor impressed with this change. Most often a second list of new excuses emerges. Be prepared! Simply begin removing the excuses from the second list and expect a third one to develop. By the time the third set of excuses is removed, there will almost always be a visible change in the indifferent partner's behavior.

- The person who loses life by following Jesus' teaching and example in a troubled marriage gains real life in Christ. Jesus teaches us to love our enemies, stand by our marriages and sacrifice ourselves in love. It's not easy, but it's often effective.

Rally around you those who can support you as you love and serve your spouse. What caring Christian people can come alongside you?

Specifically, how can your Christian friends support you? Let them know how they can support you.

How will you distinguish between winning through losing—living a life of biblical humility—and becoming a doormat or a pushover?

A painful marriage sends the faithful spouse to prayer. And prayer, sometimes coupled with fasting, leads to fresh power for God's plan of action. If the plan is big enough to call for a change in your role or your marriage relationship, it will require an appeal to your spouse. An appeal is a call for a change, or for help, or for a specific request. As you pray for your spouse and your marriage, be sensitive to when God is prompting you to make an appeal to your spouse and then act on God's prompting (see pp. 244-246). Why is each of the following directives key to making a successful appeal to your spouse?

Wise and careful timing

Tact and sensitivity

Kind words and careful phrases

Clear and polite requests

Loyalty and respect

A connection, if possible, to your spouse's interests and desires

List some issues you would like to raise with your spouse. Pray and plan how to make your appeal, using the criteria presented above.

- The only way a faithful spouse can experience positive change in his or her marriage is by putting on the full armor of God.

  Reread "Protected" on page 246 and Ephesians 6:13-20, then take an inventory of the armor you are wearing.

Is your belt of truth slipping or has it come completely unbuckled? Have you gotten into a habit of lying to avoid confrontation in your marriage? How could your honesty and integrity improve your relationship with your spouse?

What can you do every day to put on God's breastplate of righteousness rather than relying on your own flimsy self-righteousness?

What flaming arrows, or attacks from Satan, has your shield of faith recently helped you extinguish?

What are the results when you drop your shield of faith?

How can the helmet of salvation protect your mind from hurtful words and accusations? How can the assurance of your deliverance from sin—your freedom in Christ—help you deal with any difficulties with your spouse?

In what ways have you had to recently use the sword of the Spirit, God's Word? What can you do to improve your swordsmanship, that is, speaking God's Word in truth and love?

Sturdy footwear can help you stand firm and enable you to walk over rough terrain. How can the gospel of peace prepare you to walk firmly and securely through the tough territory in your marriage?

What can you do to be in a state of readiness for the difficult paths you may have to trod?

As you clothe yourself with God's armor, let your battle cry be the truth that God delights in the impossible!

QUESTIONS FOR FURTHER STUDY OR GROUP INTERACTION:

NOTES FROM GROUP INTERACTION OR PERSONAL COUNSELING:

CHAPTER FOURTEEN

Steps to Setting Your Marriage Free

The process of setting your marriage free in Christ will not work unless you speak the truth in love and walk in the light. The Lord loves you and wants to see you free from your past, alive in Him and committed to one another.

- If you haven't already done so, process the personal Steps to Freedom in Christ found in Appendix A and Chapter 14, "Steps to Setting Your Marriage Free," from *The Christ-Centered Marriage* before you begin.[1] Work through the personal steps alone or with a mature and trusted friend. Find a spot where you can read and process the steps aloud and give yourself plenty of time.

Proceed with the following material only after you have completed both sets of steps. The following activities will help both of you summarize the Steps to Setting Your Marriage Free and put what you have learned into practice.

Our God is a personal God. In what very personal ways did He touch you with healing, deliverance, insight and hope as you worked through the Steps to Freedom in Christ? Let a detailed answer to this question be your constant reminder of the Lord's work in your life and a touchstone when Satan uses circumstances to cause your faith in God to waver.

- God's will is to reveal blockages in intimacy within your marriage and to strengthen your marriage. Certainly He wants the life of Christ to display His glory in you and your marriage.

Is it your desire to walk in the light and speak the truth in love? Are you willing to allow God to show you anything He desires? If so, share your intentions with each other before you begin.

Agree to certain guidelines as you work through the Steps to Setting Your Marriage Free. You must both assume personal responsibility and not attack the other person's character or family. Allow the Holy Spirit to bring understanding and conviction. Agree to speak the truth in love and walk in the light.

- You've been laying the foundation for working through the Steps to Setting Your Marriage Free. Now take time for a little warm-up exercise. As suggested on page 252, answer the following questions:

What five character qualities do you most appreciate about
your spouse?

1.

2.

3.

4.

5.

What five things does your spouse do that you really appreciate?

1.

2.

3.

4.

5.

After sharing your answers with one another, spend a few moments in prayer. Ask God to be with you as you conclude your time working through the Steps to Setting Your Marriage Free.

Prayerfully work through the complete description in the text. When you have completed the steps in the text, answer the following questions concerning what God has taught you about Himself, about yourself, about the kind of spouse you are and about your spouse. Let your answers be a touchstone for the work of deliverance that God will do for you and your marriage.

Step One

ESTABLISH GOD'S PRIORITY FOR MARRIAGE

How completely have you left father and mother and bonded to one another? Does your spiritual heritage take precedence over your natural heritage?

In what ways could you be holding on to some unhealthy ties—physical, emotional, spiritual or financial ties—to your respective parents and not committing yourselves fully to the Lord and then to each other?

Step Two

BREAK CYCLES OF ABUSE

What habits, customs, traditions and values have you observed in your spouse's family that you really appreciate?

What iniquities and family sins of your ancestors did the Lord reveal to you?

Step Three

BALANCE RIGHTS AND RESPONSIBILITIES

How have you not loved, accepted, respected and/or submitted to your spouse?

How has your spouse shown love, appreciation, respect and acceptance to you?

Step Four

BREAK SEXUAL BONDAGE

What cleansing did you experience at this step?

Step Five

RELEASE OLD HURTS

What good memories do you share?

What will you do to build more good memories and heal the hurtful ones?

What will you do to stand strong in the forgiveness God offers you and to extend forgiveness to your spouse when the deceiver raises hurtful memories and doubts about your ability to forgive?

Step Six

UNMASK SATAN'S DECEPTIONS

What acts of deception, temptation, accusation, harassment, discouragement or disillusionment do you and your spouse frequently encounter in your marriage?

What will you do to stand strong against them?

Step Seven

RENEW CHRISTIAN MARRIAGE

What about Christian marriage were you reminded of in this step?

In the renewal of your marriage vows, what does it mean to you to become a giver instead of a taker? Be specific.

- You have won a very important battle in the ongoing war surrounding your marriage, but this freedom must be maintained.

What healthy allies do you have for your marriage? Let them know about the battle you recently fought so they can help you stand strong.

If you don't have a support group, what will you do to build one? Start this week.

What Bible study plan do you have individually and, ideally, together?

How will you encourage one another to regularly study God's Word together and individually?

What will you do to remind yourself of your identity in Christ? (See the list of truths "We Are One in Christ" on pages 280-281.)

To what Scripture verses are you clinging?

When will you review the Steps to Freedom in Christ? Schedule regular times now.

What are you doing to take every thought captive to Christ?

How will you assure that you do not revert back to old thought habits?

Again, what Scripture verses keep coming to mind?

Who do you have to hold you accountable to working on your marriage so you don't drift away from your focused effort back into old patterns of thinking?

Are you expecting your spouse to fight your battle? What are you doing to fight the battle yourself?

If necessary, which competent Christian pastor or counselor, someone committed to the biblical institution of marriage, will you turn to for help?

• It is our prayer that you have come a long way in your marriage since first opening the cover of the book and working through this study guide.

Look again at your answers to the first two questions in this guide—"Why have you picked up *The Christ-Centered Marriage*?" and "What do you hope to gain from reading this book?" Have you gained what you had hoped?

In what specific ways has your marriage been strengthened?

Take time to once again join together in the prayer found on page 279 and include some moments of giving thanks to God for the freedom in marriage that is yours through Jesus Christ.

Celebrate the blessings you have received from going through these Steps to Setting Your Marriage Free. Mark the occasion with a special time with your spouse. Plan a special evening or weekend outing to celebrate setting your marriage free!

Note:
1. Detailed instructions for working through the Steps to Setting Your Marriage Free are given in the text or you may order additional copies from Freedom in Christ, 491 East Lambert Road, La Habra, CA 90631; (562) 691-9128.

Beginning Your Marriage Free

The purpose of Beginning Your Marriage Free is to go beyond the personal Steps to Freedom in Christ by helping engaged couples resolve issues from the past that could create conflicts in their future marriage. Assuming responsibility and resolving your own issues before the Lord is the best way to prepare for marriage!

This appendix assumes that you have already read *The Christ-Centered Marriage*. In addition, reading *Victory Over the Darkness* and *The Bondage Breaker* or attending a Living Free in Christ conference will help you resolve personal and spiritual conflicts and instruct you in living the Christian life by faith in the power of the Holy Spirit. The conference is available on video- or audiocassette from Freedom in Christ Ministries.[1] Because the Steps to Freedom in Christ found in Appendix A of *The Christ-Centered Marriage* focuses on your individual relationship and identity in Christ, we encourage you to work through them before proceeding with the following steps to Beginning Your Marriage Free.

Are you willing to allow God to show you anything He desires? Is it your desire to walk in the light and speak the truth in love? Then you are ready to work through this procedure. Set aside a day and find a quiet place where you will not be disturbed. If your current courtship or marital relationship is experiencing difficulty, then we suggest that you have a responsible person whom you trust assist you in this process.

Special Note: Finding Personal Freedom in Your Marriage is designed for those who are married and desire to resolve issues which create conflict in their marriages but whose spouses are unwilling to participate in processing the Steps to Setting Your Marriage Free. Assuming your own responsibility and resolving your own issues before the Lord will bring about improvements in your marriage relationship and perhaps encourage your unwilling spouse to seek a closer relationship with you and with the Lord. The steps for Finding Personal Freedom in Your Marriage are available from Freedom in Christ Ministries.[1]

Note:
1. Detailed instructions for working through the *Steps to Setting Your Marriage Free* are given in the text or you may order additional copies from Freedom in Christ, 491 East Lambert Road, La Habra, CA 90631; (562) 691-9128.

BEFORE YOU BEGIN THE PROCESS:

You should have a Bible, some extra paper and a pen or pencil available as you work through the steps. In order to resolve conflicts, you have to address many issues that can seem negative. Therefore, begin by reflecting on the encouraging issues. Answer the following questions and later share your answers with your fiancé/fiancée:

What three character qualities do you most appreciate about your fiancé/fiancée?

1.

2.

3.

What three things does your fiancé/fiancée do that you really appreciate?

1.

2.

3.

Begin with this prayer of commitment:

> Dear Heavenly Father,
>
> I love You and thank You for Your grace, truth, love, power, forgiveness and blessings in Christ. I can love my fiancé/fiancée because You first loved me. I can forgive my fiancé/fiancée because I have been forgiven, and there can be a mutual acceptance because You have accepted us. I desire nothing more than to know and do Your will. I ask for Your divine guidance and protection during this time of seeking freedom for my future marriage.
>
> I buckle on the belt of Your truth, put on the breastplate of Your righteousness, and commit myself to the gospel of peace. I hold up the shield of faith and stand against the flaming arrows of the enemy. I commit myself to take every thought captive in obedience to You. I put on the helmet of salvation which assures me of Your forgiveness, Your life, and my freedom in You. I put off the old self and put on the new self which is being renewed in Your image. I take the sword of the Spirit, the spoken Word of God, to defend myself against the father of lies.
>
> I acknowledge my dependence on You and understand that apart from Christ I can do nothing. I pray that You will grant me genuine repentance and living faith. I desire Your plans for my

future marriage, for it to be a beautiful picture of Your relationship with the Body of Christ. I ask You to fill me with Your Holy Spirit, lead me into all truth, and set me free in Christ. In Jesus' precious name, I pray. Amen.

Step One

ESTABLISH GOD'S PRIORITY FOR MARRIAGE

Ask the Lord to reveal to you if you are prepared to leave your father and mother and be bonded only to your fiancé/fiancée. Remember the words of Jesus:

> Anyone who loves his father or mother more than me is not worthy of me; anyone who loves his son or daughter more than me is not worthy of me (Matthew 10:37).

This does not mean you shouldn't honor your father and mother, but it does mean that you can have only one Lord in your life. It means your *spiritual* heritage must take precedence over your *natural* heritage.

> For this reason a man will leave his father and mother and be united to his wife, and they will become one flesh. The man and his wife were both naked, and they felt no shame (Genesis 2: 24,25).

LEAVING

In what ways could you be holding on to some unhealthy ties that are keeping you from committing yourself fully to the Lord and to your fiancé/fiancée? Those ties could be physical, emotional, mental, spiritual or financial.

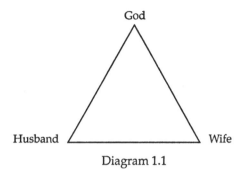

Diagram 1.1

CLEAVING (SEE DIAGRAM 1.1)

Ask the Lord to reveal to you the ways that you have not yet left your father and mother so you can cleave (be faithful) only to your fiancé/fiancée after marriage.

Pray:

> Dear Heavenly Father,
>
> I humbly submit myself to You and ask for Your divine guidance. I ask that You reveal to my mind the ways that I may allow my physical heritage to be more important than my spiritual heritage. Show me anything in my life that may take on a greater sense of importance to me than my relationship with You. I also ask You to show me what ways I am not willing to honorably leave my father and mother—physically, spiritually, mentally, emotionally or financially. I desire to be spiritually bonded to You in order that I may be fully bonded to my fiancé/fiancée in marriage. In Jesus' name, I pray. Amen.

You should sit silently before the Lord and honestly consider your relationship to God and to your own parents. Do not consider the relationship that your fiancé/fiancée has with his or her own parents. Let the Lord be the judge, and allow your fiancé/fiancée to assume responsibility for his or her relationship with his or her own parents. Consider the following questions.

CONSIDER HOW YOU RELATE TO YOUR PARENTS.

In the space provided, answer the questions and write down any thoughts that come to your mind in regard to these issues.

1. Is my relationship with God the most important relationship in my life?

2. Is my relationship with my fiancé/fiancée the second most important relationship in my life?

3. Does the approval of relatives mean more to me than the approval of God?

4. Am I still trying to live up to the expectations of my relatives?

5. Would I be willing to sever any relationship which would threaten my relationship with God even if it included my fiancé/fiancée or others of my physical family?

CONSIDER HOW YOU HONOR YOUR PARENTS.

Leaving father and mother cannot mean dishonoring them. Being disrespectful to your parents cannot lead to freedom. Consider the following questions:

1. Have you gone against your parents' counsel in planning to get married?

2. If so, have you prayerfully tried to reconcile your differences and receive their blessing?

3. In what ways have you been disrespectful of your parents?

In what ways have you not shown appreciation?

Note: If you feel your parents have wronged you, you will be given an opportunity to forgive them later in Step Five.

4. Write down any ways that you are still bonded to your own parents or stepparents in an ungodly way.

    Physically:

    Spiritually:

    Mentally:

    Emotionally:

    Financially:

When you have finished your list, privately confess your issues to God.

Later share with your fiancé/fiancée what you have learned. If it has affected your relationship with your fiancé/fiancée in a negative way, then ask him or her for forgiveness. If you have been unduly critical of your future in-laws, you should ask your fiancé/fiancée to forgive you. Conclude this step with the following prayer:

> Dear Heavenly Father,
>
> I thank You for revealing these important issues to me. I rededicate my life to You. My desire in my future marriage is to become one flesh and one spirit in Christ. May Your Holy Spirit bond me together in love for You. Show me how I can rightly relate to my earthly parents and other relatives. Thank You for Your forgiveness for any way that I have dishonored my parents, and show me how I can honor them according to Your will. In Jesus' precious name, I pray. Amen.

A note for those who have been married previously: You may need to ask the Lord if there remains any unhealthy bonding between former spouses and their families. The process would be the same as above.

Step Two

BREAK CYCLES OF ABUSE

In this step, first ask the Lord to reveal to your mind the family sins and iniquities that have been passed on to you from previous generations. Second, ask the Lord to reveal sins and wrong patterns of behavior that may affect your future marriage. Before you begin the first part, however, realize that most Christian families are just doing the very best they can, and it would be wrong to see *only* their sins and iniquities.

What habits, customs, traditions and values have you observed in your fiancé's/fiancée's family that you really appreciate?

Later, take the time to encourage your fiancé/fiancée by sharing your answer to the previous question.

Because of one man, Adam, sin entered into the world and consequently all have sinned. This transmission of sin has affected every generation and every people group of the world. The fact that there are generational cycles of abuse is a well-attested social phenomena. Here is an opportunity to find freedom in Christ by breaking the progression of ancestral sins and by making a concerted effort to stop the cycles of abuse. If we do not face these issues, we will teach what we have been taught, discipline any children we may have the way we have been disciplined, and relate to our future spouses the way our parents related to each other. Scripture teaches that those who are fully trained will be like their teachers.

Childhood training isn't just based on what was said; it's also based on what was modeled. Family values are caught more than taught.

When we were born physically alive but spiritually dead, we had neither the presence of God in our lives nor the knowledge of His ways. We have been programmed by sin to live our lives independent of God. During those formative years of our lives, we learned how to cope, survive and succeed without God. When we came to Christ, nobody pushed the "clear" button in that marvelous computer we call our mind. That is why Paul says we must no longer be conformed to this world, but be transformed by the renewing of our minds (see Romans 12:2).

We have all developed many defense mechanisms to protect ourselves. Denial, projection, blaming and many other self-protective behaviors are no longer necessary now that we are in Christ. We are accepted for who we are and that gives us the freedom to be real and honest. Jesus is our defense. We can walk in the light and speak the truth in love. We can't fix our past, but we can be free from it by the grace of God. Just trying not to be like our parents or other role models in our lives is still letting those people determine who we are and what we are doing. Thank God for the good lessons learned, but let the Lord renew your mind and become free from what was not right in your past.

Strongholds have been erected in your mind by the environment in which you were raised and the traumatic experiences in your past. Those strongholds affect your temperament and the way you relate to your fiancé/fiancée and future children. Strongholds result in deeply set patterns of behavior that will remain unless we renew our minds according to the Word of God.

> Ah, Sovereign LORD, you have made the heavens and the earth by your great power and outstretched arm. Nothing is too hard for you. You show love to thousands but bring the punishment for the fathers' sins into the laps of their children after them (Jeremiah 32:17,18).

IDENTIFYING GENERATIONAL SINS

Start this step by asking the Lord to mentally reveal the iniquities and family sins of your ancestors passed on spiritually and environmentally.

Pray the following prayer:

> Dear Heavenly Father,
>
> You are the only perfect parent I have. Thank You for my natural parents who brought me into this world. I acknowledge that they were not perfect, nor was my family and community where I grew up. I ask that You reveal to my mind the dysfunctional patterns and family sins of my ancestors that have been going on for generations. Reveal to me the strongholds in my mind that have kept me from fully honoring You and embracing the truth. Give me the grace to face the truth and not to be defensive. Only You can meet my deepest needs of acceptance, security, significance and a sense of belonging. I thank You that You have made me a new creation in Christ. I desire to be free from my past so I can be all that You want me to be. In Jesus' name, I pray. Amen.

Allow the Lord to reveal any and all family sins of your ancestors. Considering your own upbringing and family heritage, honestly answer the following questions:

1. What sins seemed to be repeated over and over again in your family, such as lying, criticizing, drinking, compulsive gambling, cheating, pride, bitterness, adultery, divorce, incest, sexual abuse, etc.?

2. How did your family deal with conflict?

   How do you now deal with it?

3. How did each member of your family communicate? Can you speak the truth in love?

4. How did your parents discipline their children?

   How will you?

5. Where did your parents get their significance?

Security?

Acceptance?

Where do you?

6. Did your parents exhibit the spiritual fruit of self-control or were they controllers or enablers? Which are you?

7. What was their religious preference?

What non-Christian beliefs—cultic or occultic—or idols did they embrace? (An idol can be anything that has greater prominence in their lives than Christ.)

8. What lies did they believe?

How has this affected you?

9. What other ancestral sins has God revealed to your mind?

Later share what you have learned from your list with your fiancé/fiancée. Knowing that you are willing to face these issues will give you and your fiancé/fiancée a lot more hope for the future. Remember, "there is now no condemnation for those who are in Christ Jesus" (Romans 8:1), and we are to accept one another as Christ has accepted us (see Romans 15:7). Mutual sharing allows both of you to understand and accept each other.

We are not responsible for our parents' sins, but because our parents sinned, we have been taught, trained and disciplined in ways that may not be healthy. Denial and cover-up will only perpetuate the sins of our ancestors and affect us and our future children. It is our responsibility to face these issues and stop the cycle of abuse so it is not passed on to the next generation. The Lord instructs us to confess our iniquity and the iniquity of our forefathers (see Leviticus 26:40).

Pray the following prayer for every family sin of your ancestors that you have written down.

> Dear Heavenly Father,
> I confess (name every sin) as sinful and displeasing to You. Thank You for Your forgiveness. I now turn from those sins, reject them, and ask You to break their hold on my future marriage. In Jesus' name, I pray. Amen.

CURRENT PATTERNS IN COURTSHIP

We are to confess not only the family sins of our ancestors but also our own sins. Individual sins are dealt with in the personal Steps to Freedom in Christ. However, dating/courting relationships also have corporate sins which must be confessed and forsaken. Corporate sins are patterns of behavior in dating/courting relationships that are displeasing to God and contrary to His revealed will. They do not differ from individual sins in nature. Sin is still sin whether practiced by an individual or by a couple. A pattern of sinfulness within a dating/courting relationship should be dealt with before you get married or it will continue on into marriage.

Examples of corporate sins in dating/courting relationships might be:

1. Engaging together in sinful activities that displease God or damage others;

2. Taking part together in non-Christian religious rituals or any cult or occult ceremonies or practices;

3. Agreeing together on any sin: covering up for each other, lying, theft, fornication, divorce, drunkenness, child abuse, etc.;

4. Withholding tithes and offerings from God;

5. Falling into patterns of gossip, slander, filthy language or other sins of the tongue in conversations with each other;

6. Tolerating sinful behavior in your families and friends, especially while they live under your roof, such as swearing, foul language, sex outside of marriage, gambling, alcohol, drugs, or anything that contradicts God's written Word;

7. Reading or viewing pornographic material or anything produced by psychics, mediums, occult practitioners, cults or false religions.

Pray the following prayer:

> Dear Heavenly Father,
> As I seek You, bring to my mind all the corporate sins that I have committed in my courting relationship and family. Remind me of the sins of my ancestors and their families. Open my eyes to any tendency to repeat the same dysfunctional patterns. Give me discernment to identify and renounce corporate sins with my fiancé/fiancée that I have tolerated or have not dealt with adequately. Then grant me Your grace that I may confess them, renounce them and turn away from them so I may commit myself never to return to them. In Jesus' cleansing name, I pray. Amen.

Identify any corporate sins the Holy Spirit has brought to your mind and write them down on a separate sheet of paper. Confess all that the Lord has revealed to you. Once you have completed this step, destroy the paper on which you have written these sins.

At a later time, ask your fiancé's/fiancée's forgiveness for the ways that your involvement in these sins has hurt him or her and damaged your relationship together. If your fiancé/fiancée is reluctant to participate with you in this sharing, then share with him or her how the Lord has convicted you in what you have been doing. With firmness and love say that you are no longer willing to be a part of these actions. Should your fiancé/fiancée not accept you for making a stand for righteousness' sake, then it is best to find that out before you are married.

When finished, make the following declaration aloud:

> I confess and renounce my own corporate sins and all those sins of my ancestors. I declare by the grace of God that I am a new creation in Christ. I commit myself and my future marriage to the Lord Jesus Christ. I take my place in Christ and by His authority I command Satan to flee from me and my relationship with my fiancé/fiancée (and our family relationships). I belong to God, and am a part of His family and under His protection. I put on the armor of God and commit myself to stand firm in my relationship to my heavenly Father.

Satan's grip from generational sins and cycles of abuse can be broken instantly. However, it will take time to renew our minds and overcome patterns of the flesh. An experienced pastor or committed Christian counselor can often help in this process. We must accept one another and build up one another. Growth in character will also take time and we must be patient with each other. Unconditional love and acceptance frees individuals so they can accept themselves and grow in the grace of the Lord.

Conclude this step with the following prayer:

Dear Heavenly Father,

Thank You for Your unconditional love and acceptance. I give myself to You. Enable me by Your grace to accept my fiancé/fiancée as You have accepted me, and to be merciful as You have been merciful. Show me how we can build up, encourage and forgive each other. I acknowledge that I have not attained the full stature of Christ, but I desire to be like You in my future marriage and in all I do.

I face up to my own corporate sins, as well as the family sins of my ancestors. I honestly confess my participation in them and agree that this behavior is unacceptable to You. I disown them and repudiate them. In Jesus' name, I break all the influence of their dysfunctional patterns upon me and my future marriage. I cancel out all advantages, schemes and other works of the devil that have been passed to me from my ancestors. I break any foothold or stronghold built from the enemy's influence and I give my heart to You for the renewing of my mind.

I invite the Holy Spirit to apply the shed blood of the Lord Jesus on Calvary's cross to my corporate sins and to my ancestral sins. Through God's grace, by faith, I claim the work of Christ in His death and resurrection as my ransom from sin, release from guilt and removal of shame. In Jesus' precious name, I pray. Amen.

Step Three

BALANCE RIGHTS AND RESPONSIBILITIES

In this step ask the Lord to reveal to your mind any ways that you have not related to your fiancé/fiancée in a godly way.

Do nothing out of selfish ambition or vain conceit, but in humility consider others better than yourselves. Each of you should look not only to your own interests, but also to the interests of others. Your attitude should be the same as that of Christ Jesus (Philippians 2:3-5). Who are you to judge someone else's servant? To his own master he stands or falls. And he will stand, for the Lord is able to make him stand (Romans 14:4).

The following is a list of the languages of love from *The Five Love Languages* by Gary Chapman. If you do not remember what each language means, you may want to read or review Chapter 8 in *The Christ-Centered Marriage* before completing this activity. Read over the list and write 1 beside the way you tend to show love to others; write 2 beside the way you like to have love shown to you; write 3 beside the way your fiancé/fiancée shows love to you; and write 4 beside the way you tend to show love to your fiancé/fiancée.

_____	Gifts
_____	Service
_____	Time
_____	Touch
_____	Words

What personal needs do you feel are not being met in your life? (For example, you don't feel loved, accepted, appreciated, etc.)

Caution: Do not attack your fiancé's/fiancée's character or suggest what he or she should or should not do. That is his or her responsibility.

Complete the following statements to reinforce your fiancé's/fiancée's attempts to love you:

1. I really feel loved when he or she does or says...

2. I really feel accepted when he or she does or says…

3. I really feel respected when he or she does or says…

4. I really feel appreciated when he or she does or says…

Scripture teaches that we are to be submissive to one another's needs, which include loving, accepting and respecting one another. Pray the following prayer, asking the Lord to reveal any ways that self-centered living and demanding your own rights have kept you from assuming your responsibilities to love and accept your fiancé/fiancée.

> Dear Heavenly Father,
> Thank You for Your full and complete love and acceptance. Thank You that the unselfish sacrifice of Christ's death on the cross and His resurrection have met my greatest need for forgiveness and life. I ask You to reveal to my mind any ways that I have been selfish in my relationship with my fiancé/fiancée. Show me how I have not loved, accepted or respected him or her in the fear of Christ. Show me how I have been angry, jealous, insecure, manipulative or controlling. In Jesus' name, I pray. Amen.

Sit silently before the Lord and allow Him to reveal any and all ways that you have not in word or deed…

1. Loved your fiancé/fiancée as you should have (see Ephesians 5:22; Titus 2:4,5).

2. Accepted your fiancé/fiancée as you should have (see Romans 15:7).

3. Respected your fiancé/fiancée as you should have (see Ephesians 5:33).

4. Appreciated your fiancé/fiancée as you should have (see 1 Peter 3:1-9).

5. Trusted God to bring conviction and self-control in your fiancé/fiancée (see John 16:8; Galatians 5:23).

When you have completed the above, verbally confess what the Lord has shown you.

Later ask your fiancé's/fiancée's forgiveness for not being what God called you to be. Don't overlook the times and ways that you have communicated rejection, disrespect or shown lack of appreciation. Now share your own personal needs that you feel are not being met (without attacking the other person's character or telling him or her what he or she should or shouldn't do). Then share the times and the ways that your fiancé/fiancée has shown love, acceptance, respect and appreciation to you.

Conclude this step with the following prayer of commitment:

> Dear Heavenly Father,
>
> I have fallen short of Your glory and have not lived up to my responsibilities. I have been selfish and self-centered. Thank You for Your forgiveness. I commit myself to an increasing pattern of love, acceptance and respect for my fiancé/fiancée. In Jesus' name, I pray. Amen.

Step Four

BREAK SEXUAL BONDAGE

> **Note:** Before you begin Step Four, *individual* freedom from sexual bondage must be achieved. You should have already dealt with your individual issues in Step Six: Bondage vs. Freedom in the Steps to Freedom in Christ. If you have not dealt with them, Step Six: Bondage vs. Freedom is provided here, following Step Four.
>
> As mentioned in the introduction, everyone is strongly encouraged to work through the individual Steps to Freedom in Christ for the complete process.

Sexual purity:

For this is the will of God, your sanctification; that is, that you abstain from sexual immorality; that each of you know how to possess his own vessel in sanctification and honor, not in lustful passion, like the Gentiles who do not know God (1 Thessalonians 4:3-5, *NASB*).

Sexual need:

The husband should fulfill his marital duty to his wife, and likewise the wife to her husband. The wife's body does not belong to her alone but also to her husband. In the same way, the husband's body does not belong to him alone but also to his wife. Do not deprive each other except by mutual consent and for a time, so that you may devote yourselves to prayer (1 Corinthians 7:3-5).

Sexual honor:

> Marriage should be honored by all, and the marriage bed kept pure, for God will judge the adulterer and all the sexually immoral (Hebrews 13:4).

Sexual lust:

> But I tell you that anyone who looks at a woman lustfully has already committed adultery with her in his heart (Matthew 5:28).

A person cannot personally resolve a problem of lust; only Christ can break that bondage. Be sure to read Chapter 10 in *The Christ-Centered Marriage* before you proceed. Many have found great encouragement by reading *A Way of Escape* (Neil Anderson) and *Running the Red Lights* (Charles Mylander) which share how Jesus Christ is the answer for those struggling with sexual bondage. Individual sexual freedom must be achieved first before you can meet one another's sexual needs in marriage.

Consider areas where you may have opened the door to the enemy and brought bondage to your relationship. These questions need to be honestly answered and forgiveness sought.

1. In what ways have you not been honest in your relationship with your fiancé/fiancée?

2. What have you been doing together that you now think to be wrong?

3. How has your conscience been violated or have you violated the conscience of the other?

At a later time, be sure you cover any forgiveness issues with your fiancé/fiancée. The best way to find out if you have violated the other person's conscience is to ask!

Complete this step with the following prayer:

> Dear Heavenly Father,
>
> I stand before You acknowledging that You know the thoughts and intentions of my heart. I desire to be sexually free before You. I acknowledge that I have sinned and thank You for Your forgiveness and cleansing. I now give my body to You and reserve its sexual use for marriage only. Fill me with Your Holy Spirit and bond me together in love in the right way and at the right time. May my sexual relationship be holy in Your sight. In Jesus' name, I pray. Amen.

Then declare aloud:

> In the name and authority of the Lord Jesus Christ, I command Satan to leave my presence. I present my body to the Lord Jesus Christ and reserve its sexual use for my future marriage only.

If you have been inappropriately involved with your fiancé/fiancée sexually prior to marriage, pray the following aloud:

> Dear Heavenly Father,
>
> I know that You desire for me to be free from sexual bondage and to be righteously responsive and respectful of my fiancé's/fiancée's needs. Free me from my lust and show me how we can relate to each other in honest love and respect.

I now ask You to reveal to my mind any way that
I have sexually sinned in our relationship. Give
me the grace to face the truth. In Jesus' precious
name, I pray. Amen.

Sit silently before the Lord and allow Him to guide you. Ask
Him to cover these next few minutes with grace. Sex is a very
intimate expression of love and can be a tremendous cause for
guilt and insecurity when experienced outside the will of God.

The following is for those needing to work through Step Six of
Steps to Freedom in Christ.

BONDAGE VS. FREEDOM
(STEP SIX FROM THE STEPS TO FREEDOM IN CHRIST)

It is our responsibility not to allow sin to have control over our
bodies. We must not use our bodies or another person's body
as an instrument of unrighteousness (see Romans 6:12,13). If
you are struggling with sexual sins that you cannot stop—
such as pornography, masturbation, sexual immorality—then
pray as follows:

Lord,
I ask You to bring to my mind every sexual use
of my body as an instrument of unrighteousness
so I can renounce these sins right now. In Jesus'
name, I pray. Amen.

As the Lord brings to your mind every wrong sexual use of
your body, whether it was done to you—rape, incest, sexual
molestation—or willingly by you, *renounce every occasion:*

Lord,
I renounce (name the specific use of your body)
with (name any other person involved) and I ask
You to break that sinful bond with (name).

After you are finished, commit your body to the Lord by praying:

> Lord,
>
> I renounce all these uses of my body as an instrument of unrighteousness and I admit to my willful participation. I choose now to present my eyes, mouth, mind, heart, hands, feet and sexual organs to You as instruments of righteousness. I present my whole body to You as a living sacrifice, holy and acceptable, and I choose to reserve the sexual use of my body for marriage only (see Hebrews 13:4).
>
> I reject the devil's lie that my body is not clean or that it is dirty or in any way unacceptable to You as a result of my past sexual experiences. Lord, thank You that You have totally cleansed and forgiven me and that You love and accept me just the way I am. Therefore, I choose now to accept myself and my body as clean in Your eyes. Amen.

After you have confessed all known sin, pray:

> Lord,
>
> I now confess these sins to You and claim through the blood of the Lord Jesus Christ my forgiveness and cleansing. I cancel out all ground that evil spirits have gained through my willful involvement in sin. I pray this in the wonderful name of my Lord and Savior, Jesus Christ. Amen.

Step Five

RELEASE OLD HURTS

Forgiveness is what sets us free from our past. It is routinely necessary in any relationship because we don't live with perfect people. Resentment and bitterness will tear us apart. Forgiveness is the first step in reconciliation, which is essential for bonding together. We also need to forgive others so Satan cannot take advantage of us (see 2 Corinthians 2:10,11). We are to be merciful just as our heavenly Father is merciful (see Luke 6:36). We are to forgive as we have been forgiven (see Ephesians 4:32).

Start this step by making a time line, beginning with the day you first met your fiancé/fiancée and ending with today. Above the line, list all the good memories that you have had together. Below the line, list all the painful memories.

Good Memories

When We First Met _____ Today

Painful Memories

Thank the Lord for the good memories that have been especially meaningful in your relationship:

> Lord,
> I thank you for (name the good memory).

After thanking the Lord aloud for the good memories, pray the following prayer:

> Dear Heavenly Father,
> Sometimes pain has come to me through circumstances, sometimes from other people, sometimes from my fiancé/fiancée. Whatever the cause, surface in my mind all the pain that You want me to deal with at this time. Let me get in touch with the emotional core of my hurt and heartache, trauma and threat that has damaged my relationship with my fiancé/fiancée. Show me where I have allowed a root of bitterness to spring up, causing trouble and defiling many. In Jesus' precious name, I pray. Amen.

Spend a few moments in silent prayer, allowing the Lord to help you recall the painful experiences and traumatic events of your dating/courting relationship.

List the names of all those who have hurt you in any way, including all those for whom you have bad feelings:

Using a separate sheet of paper, make a list of the painful memories the Lord brings to your mind. Use real names, places and dates as much as possible. It is nearly impossible to get in touch with the emotional core of pain without using people's names and recalling specific events.

It is easy to pick up each other's offenses. It is also easy to turn bitter toward those whom you perceive to have wrongly influenced your fiancé/fiancée, even when he or she doesn't see it. Jealousy can also create bitterness.

Realize that this is a time to bring healing to damaged emotions so you can be free from your past. Simply record what happened and how you felt about it. Understand that forgiveness is not forgetting. Forgiveness may lead to forgetting, but trying to forget only complicates forgiveness. Before you start the forgiveness process, please recall these ten steps to forgiveness:

1. Allow yourself to feel the pain, hurt, resentment, bitterness and hate (see Matthew 5:4).
2. Submit to God, recalling how Christ forgave you (see Matthew 18:21-35; Ephesians 4:32; Colossians 3:13; James 4:7,8).
3. Ask for Christ's grace and power to forgive (see Luke 11:9,10).
4. Agree to live with the unavoidable consequences of the other person's sin against you (see Ephesians 5:21; Colossians 3:13).
5. Release the offense. Tear up the moral, personal, or relational debt owed you (see Matthew 6:12).
6. Never bring up a past offense again as a weapon against your fiancé/fiancée (see Romans 12:17).
7. Keep forgiving when your emotions recycle the pain or when the other person keeps offending you (see Matthew 18:21,22).
8. Reject the sinful act and tolerate it no longer (see Romans 12:21).
9. Turn the vengeance over to God and over to God's human authorities (see Romans 12:19,20).
10. Replace the old resentful feelings with the forgiving love of Christ (see Ephesians 4:31,32).

Do not make forgiveness more difficult than it already is. Some things we don't have to do:

1. We don't have to feel good about the person who hurt us—either before or after we forgive.
2. We don't have to tell the offender or other people about our resentful feelings unless the Holy Spirit guides us to do so. Jesus tells us in Matthew 5:23-26 to seek forgiveness and be reconciled to those we have offended as the Holy Spirit would guide.
3. We don't have to wait until we feel like forgiving. We can choose to obey God's Word right now.

Lift your painful memories before the Lord, asking for courage to face the pain honestly and for the grace to forgive fully. Releasing the offense results in relieving the pain.

Item by item, forgive each person you recall and release the offense as follows:

> Lord,
> I forgive (name) for (specifically identify all offenses and painful memories).

Prayerfully focus on each person until every remembered pain has surfaced. Be sure to include your fiancé/fiancée and every painful memory in your courtship. You should also accept God's forgiveness of yourself as needed. Bitterness hardens the heart, but forgiveness softens it.

After you have completed the above, pray the following prayer aloud:

> Dear Heavenly Father,
> I thank You for Your unconditional love and forgiveness. It is Your kindness and patience that have led me to forgiveness. In the name of Jesus and with His kindness and tenderness, I forgive every person who has ever hurt me or my family. I forgive my fiancé/fiancée for the pain that has come through weakness, poor judgment and

outright sin. I accept Your forgiveness for the pain and damage caused in my relationship with him or her.

By your grace bring healing, help and hope to those who have hurt me and to those who have been hurt by me. I bless them all in the name of our Lord Jesus Christ, who taught us, "'Love your enemies, do good to those who hate you, bless those who curse you, and pray for those who mistreat you'" (Luke 6:27,28). According to your Word, I pray for those who have hurt me. In the precious name of Jesus Christ, amen.

Make the following declaration aloud:

By the authority of the Lord Jesus Christ, who is seated at the heavenly Father's right hand, I assume my responsibility to resist the devil. I declare that I am crucified, buried, made alive, raised up and seated with Christ at the right hand of God. In union with Christ and with His authority, I command Satan to release any and all footholds in my life or any influence on my relationship with my fiancé/fiancée as we contemplate our future marriage. Satan, in the all-powerful Name of the crucified, risen and reigning Lord Jesus Christ, leave my presence. Do not come back. Take away with you all of your lingering effects upon our memories, our relationships, our present thoughts and our future together.

Step Six

UNMASKING SATAN'S DECEPTIONS

> Finally, be strong in the Lord and in his mighty
> power. Put on the full armor of God so that you
> can take your stand against the devil's schemes.
> For our struggle is not against flesh and blood,
> but against the rulers, against the authorities,
> against the powers of this dark world and against
> the spiritual forces of evil in the heavenly realms
> (Ephesians 6:10-12).

The goal of Satan is to discredit the work of Christ and tear
apart your *relationship,* future marriage and family. His primary weapons are deception, temptation and accusation. He also
uses harassment, discouragement and disillusionment. When
we buy his little lies, we turn against God and each other. Our
homes can become battlegrounds instead of proving grounds.
In our relationships, our desire should be that we're a vital
part of the building crew, rather than the wrecking crew. The
tongue, however, is the instrument Satan uses the most. We
either become tongue-tied and refuse to speak the truth in
love, or we allow the tongue to become a destructive weapon.

If only one member of a family pays attention to the Holy
Spirit, it can have strengthening effects upon every other
member. On the other hand, if only one member of a family
pays attention to a deceiving spirit, it can have weakening
effects upon every other member as well. The purpose of this
step is to unmask the evil one's deceptions and stand against
his attacks in the power of the Holy Spirit.

Satan uses real people to mount his attacks. They may come
from deceived or evil people inside or outside our families. For example, a friend or coworker may lead your
fiancé/fiancée into a sexual affair. The attacks may come
through relatives or neighbors who use their tongues as
destructive weapons. They may come from people who give

us bad counsel concerning marriage. They may even possibly come through satanists who use occultic rituals or blood sacrifices in an evil attempt to destroy our families and, therefore, our testimonies.

Ask the Lord to show you the nature of these attacks so you can stand against them, united as one under the lordship of Christ.

Pray the following prayer:

> Dear Heavenly Father,
>
> I stand under Your authority. I give thanks that You are my hiding place, my protection and my refuge. In the name of Jesus, I clothe myself with the full armor of God. I choose to be strong in You, Lord, and in the power of Your might. I stand firm in my faith, I submit to You and I resist the devil.
>
> Open my eyes that I may see the attacks of the evil one against me, my family, and my future marriage. Give me spiritual discernment to become aware of Satan's schemes, not ignorant of them. Open my eyes to the reality of the spiritual world in which I live. I ask You for the ability to discern spiritually so I can judge rightly between good and evil.
>
> As I wait silently before You, reveal to me the attacks of Satan against me, my family, my future marriage and my ministry in order that I may stand against them and expose the father of lies. In Jesus' discerning name, I pray. Amen.

Make a list of whatever God brings to your mind. Look for patterns that seem to repeat themselves, such as conflicts that always break out before church, prayer or discussions on spiritual things. Think of any unresolved conflicts which keep recurring that may be due to one of the following three areas:

1. Repeating mental thoughts that cause you to close your spirit toward God and your fiancé/fiancée (see 2 Corinthians 10:3-5; 1 Timothy 4:1):

2. Recurring times or situations that cause distraction, confusion and disorientation in your relationship and home (usually during discussions, devotions and times surrounding church or ministry opportunities; see 1 Thessalonians 2:18):

3. Improper stewardship (see 1 Corinthians 4:1,2):
   a. Sins that were tolerated in your home

   b. Anti-Christian objects brought into your home

Sinful activities need to be renounced. Attacks that come from the enemy because of our obedience to Christ need to be understood so we can recognize them and stand against them in the future. You need to understand how you wrestle not against flesh and blood, but against the powers of darkness (see Ephesians 6:12). Don't be like a blindfolded warrior who strikes out at himself or others. When you tear down a satanic stronghold, you will have some resistance. In order to walk free from past influences and present attacks, verbally make the following declaration:

> As a child of God who has been delivered from the power of darkness and translated into the kingdom of God's dear Son, I submit to God and resist the devil. I cancel out all demonic working that has been passed on to me from my ancestors. I have been crucified and raised with my Lord Jesus Christ, and now sit enthroned with Him in heavenly places. I renounce all satanic assignments that are directed toward me, my family, my ministry or my future marriage. I cancel every curse that Satan and his deceived, misguided evil workers have put on me and on God's plan for my future marriage. I announce to Satan and all his forces that Christ became a curse for me when He died on the cross.
>
> I reject any and every way in which Satan may claim ownership of me. I belong to the Lord Jesus Christ who purchased me with His own blood. I reject all other occultic rituals and blood sacrifices whereby Satan may claim ownership of me and God's plan for my future marriage. I declare myself to be eternally and completely signed over and committed to the Lord Jesus Christ. By the authority I have in Jesus Christ, I now command every enemy of the Lord Jesus Christ to leave my presence, my memory and my present thoughts. I commit myself to our Heavenly Father to do His will from this day forward.

Then pray:

> Dear Heavenly Father,
>
> I come to You as Your child, purchased by the blood of the Lord Jesus Christ. You are the Lord of the universe and the Lord of my life. I yield my rights to You as the Lord of my future marriage. I submit my body to You as an instrument of

righteousness, a living sacrifice, that I may glorify You in my body and in my future marriage. I reserve the sexual use of my body for marriage only. I now ask You to fill me with Your Holy Spirit. I commit myself to the renewing of my mind in order to prove that Your will is good, perfect and acceptable for me. I commit myself to take every thought captive to the obedience of Christ. All this I do in the name and authority of the Lord Jesus Christ. Amen.

Next, you need to commit the place you live to the Lord.

Have you brought any foreign objects into your home that could serve as an idol or objects that were ever used for non-Christian religious purposes? These could provide grounds for Satan to have access to your home. Are there any pornographic videos, magazines or books, occultic or false religion materials? Is there anything else that needs to be cleansed from your home? Ask the Lord to reveal any such sins or articles in your home.

Covenant before the Lord to remove all these items from your home and burn or destroy them. Then commit your home in prayer to the Lord as follows:

Dear Heavenly Father,
I acknowledge that You are the Lord of all. All things You have created are good. You have charged me to be a good steward of all that You have entrusted to me. Thank You for what You have provided for me. I claim no ownership of

what You have entrusted to me. I dedicate my future home to You, my present living quarters, my work space, and all the property, possessions and finances You have entrusted to me. I promise to remove from my home anything and everything that displeases You.

I renounce any attacks, devices or ceremonies of the enemy or his people designed to claim any ownership of that with which I have been entrusted. I have been bought and purchased by the blood sacrifice of the Lord Jesus Christ. I claim my current home and my future home as a place of spiritual safety and protection from the evil one. I renounce anything and everything not pleasing to our Heavenly Father which has taken place in my home by me or by those who have lived there before me. I ask for Your divine protection around my home. I desire to honor You in all my ways. Thank You for Your protection.

Lord, You are the King of my life and I desire the plans that You have for my future marriage. May all that I do bring honor and glory to You. In Jesus' holy name, I pray. Amen.

Then declare aloud:

As a child of God, seated with Christ in the heavenly places, I command every evil spirit to leave my presence and my home. I renounce all attacks against my house, property, possessions and my very life. I announce to Satan and all his workers that God's plan for my future marriage, family and all that my Heavenly Father has entrusted to me belongs to the Lord Jesus Christ. I submit completely to the direction and guidance of the Holy Spirit.

Step Seven

CHRISTIAN MARRIAGE

All who marry, whether Christian or not, become part of God's creation order of marriage (see Genesis 1:26-28; 2:18-25). A *creation order* is a God-given longing built into the fabric of human life. As a result of this God-given longing, every culture and people group on earth practice marriage in some form. No exceptions! Violating marriage breaks the order of creation and always brings terrible consequences.

When one partner (or both) knows Jesus Christ as Lord and Savior, their marriage becomes a sanctified—or set apart as holy—part of God's new Christian order (see 1 Corinthians 7:14). They commit themselves to Christ's new creation in marriage and enter a marriage covenant before God and one another. Christian marriage far exceeds a mere social contract. Marriage as a social contract is only a legal agreement between two parties. Christian marriage is a lifelong covenant with binding vows, spoken before God and human witnesses. If the vows are broken, they bring God's judgment. If they are kept, they bring God's rewards.

Satan's lie is that people who marry are really married singles, bound only by a human relationship and a social contract. That means marriage can be broken whenever either party feels the partners have "irreconcilable differences." In Christ, there are no irreconcilable differences. We have been reconciled to Him and we have been given the ministry of reconciliation.

God's truth is that marriage vows bind us into the organic union of Christian marriage, a new creation that lasts until the death of one of the spouses. A contract can be canceled, but a Christian covenant lasts a lifetime. Contracts can be broken or renegotiated, but a new creation in Christ either grows toward fulfillment or is violated.

Living in obedience to God's Word in Christian marriage, as in any other part of life, brings the Lord's shelter of protection (see Psalm 91). It results in God's blessings, including children who are set apart for God's purposes (see 1 Corinthians 7:14). By God's grace His blessings extend not only to those who are faithful to Him, but also to their descendants for many generations to come (see Exodus 20:6; Deuteronomy 7:9; Luke 1:50). Violating marriage vows brings God's curse, not only upon ourselves, but also upon our descendants for three or four generations (see Exodus 34:7; Numbers 14:18; Jeremiah 32:18).

Declare aloud:

> I submit myself to God's plan for my future marriage. Satan, I renounce you in all your works and all your ways. In the all-powerful name of the Lord Jesus Christ, I command you to leave me. Take all your deceitful spirits, evil demons and fallen angels with you, and go to the place where the Lord Jesus Christ sends you. Leave my fiancé/fiancée and me and don't come back. Take with you all of your temptations. Take with you all of your accusing and demeaning thoughts that have been raised up against the knowledge of God and toward us. Take with you all of your deceptions that contradict God's written Word. The Lord Jesus Christ has torn down your demonic authority and I stand against your influence and activity toward my life and for my future marriage.
>
> You are a defeated foe, disarmed of your weapons and made a public spectacle by the cross and resurrection of Christ (see Colossians 2:15). He (God) that is in me is greater than you who are in the world (see 1 John 4:4). You, as prince of this world, now stand condemned (see John 16:11). Christ has the supremacy over every evil throne, power, rule or authority (see Colossians 1:16). Jesus shared our humanity so that by His death He might destroy him who holds the power of death—that is, the devil (see Hebrews 2:14). I resist you by the authority of Christ and because I am alive in Him; therefore, you must flee from me (see James 4:7).

Pray aloud:

> Dear Heavenly Father,
>
> I gladly acknowledge that You created marriage and family life for Your glory. Thank You for designing marriage as a "creation order," woven

into the fabric of human society. I commit myself anew to honor the covenant of Christian marriage with all its blessings.

I renounce the lie of the devil that we are to be nothing more than married singles, bound only by a human relationship and a social contract. I choose to believe that marriage is binding as long as we both shall live. I acknowledge that we can never violate our marriage vows without bringing lasting damage upon ourselves and our future descendants for three or four generations to come.

I confess that I have fallen short of Your perfect will by my own selfishness and sin. I gladly accept Your forgiveness of my sins through the blood of Christ on the cross (see 1 John 2:1,2). By grace through faith I receive Christ's abundant life into my heart and His holiness into my life (see John 10:10; 1 Corinthians 7:14).

I crucify my own fleshly lusts and sinful desires which tempt me to ignore or violate my future marriage vows (see Galatians 5:24; 1 Peter 2:11). I clothe myself and Your plans for my coming marriage with the Lord Jesus Christ and His armor of light (see Romans 13:12-14; Galatians 3:26,27). I give myself to live by the power of the Holy Spirit in daily obedience to Christ (see Galatians 5:16; 1 Peter 1:2).

I announce that in Christ I have all the spiritual blessings I need to live out my new creation and the Christian covenant of marriage. I affirm that I can become one in Christ Jesus—one marriage, one flesh, one family (see Genesis 2:24; Mark 10:6-9; Ephesians 1:3; 3:14,15). I submit myself and God's plan for my future marriage to the ownership of my Heavenly Father, to the Lordship of Jesus Christ, and to the power of the Holy Spirit. From this day forward, I ask You to use Your plans for my future marriage to display Your splendor before our families and friends. I invite You to work through us to show Your glory in the midst of a corrupt and wicked generation. In Jesus' glorious name, amen.

LIVING FREE IN CHRIST

Know that both marriage intimacy and freedom must be maintained. In gaining your freedom, you have won a very important battle in an ongoing war. And freedom is yours as long as you keep choosing truth and standing firm in the strength of the Lord. If more painful memories should surface, or if you become aware of lies that you have been living, renounce them and choose the truth. If you haven't already done so, please read *Victory over the Darkness* and *The Bondage Breaker*. *Walking in the Light* was written to help people understand God's guidance so they are able to discern counterfeit guidance. In order to maintain your freedom, we suggest the following:

1. Become active in a Christ-centered church, a small Christian group and a ministry for Christ. Build healthy allies for your coming marriage. Step outside of yourself for Christ.

2. Study your Bible daily, pray and be sensitive to the leading of the Holy Spirit. We also suggest reading one chapter of *Living Free in Christ* together every day for the next 36 days. Then use the devotional, *Daily in Christ*, by Neil and Joanne Anderson.

3. Review and apply your personal freedom in Christ. Remind yourself of your identity in Christ, winning the battle for the mind and processing the Steps to Freedom in Christ as an ongoing personal inventory. Realize that the Lord will use marriage to reveal more layers of our selfishness which He wants to peel off like the layers of an onion.

4. Take every thought captive to the obedience of Christ. Assume responsibility for private thoughts, reject the lie, choose the truth and stand firm in your identity in Christ.

5. Don't drift away! It is very easy to get lazy in your thoughts and revert back to old habit patterns of thinking. Share struggles openly with each other. See the suggested daily prayer.

6. Don't expect your fiancé/fiancée to fight your battles. While you can help each other, no one else can think, pray or read the Bible for you.

7. If serious problems surface in your relationship, seek out a competent Christian pastor or counselor who is committed to the biblical institution of marriage and not just to the individual apart from marriage.

Pray daily with confidence as follows:

Dear Heavenly Father,

I honor You as my sovereign Lord. I acknowledge that You are always present with me. You are the only all-powerful and all-wise God. You are kind and loving in all Your ways. I love You. I thank You that I am united with Christ and am spiritually alive in Him. I choose not to love the world and I crucify the flesh and all its sinful desires.

I thank You that I am a child of God, a new creation in Christ Jesus, dead to sin but alive to God. I ask You to fill me with Your Holy Spirit that I may live my life free from sin. I declare my dependence upon You and take my stand against Satan and all his lying ways. I choose to believe the truth. You are the God of all hope and I am confident that You will meet my needs as I seek to live according to Your Word. I express with confidence that I can live a responsible life and be faithful in my coming marriage through Christ who strengthens me. I ask these things in the precious name of my Lord and Savior, Jesus Christ. Amen.

Declaration:

I now take my stand in Christ and put on the whole armor of God. In union with Christ, I command Satan and all his evil spirits to depart from me. I submit my body to God as a living sacrifice and I renew my mind by the living Word of God in order that I may prove that the will of God is good, acceptable and perfect.

Use the following list to celebrate who you are in Christ:

IN CHRIST

I AM ACCEPTED

John 1:12	I am God's child.
John 15:15	I am Christ's friend.
Romans 5:1	I have been justified.
1 Corinthians 6:17	I am united with the Lord, and I am one spirit with Him.
1 Corinthians 6:20	I have been bought with a price. I belong to God.
1 Corinthians 12:27	I am a member of Christ's body.
Ephesians 1:1	I am a saint.
Ephesians 1:5	I have been adopted as God's child.
Ephesians 2:18	I have direct access to God through the Holy Spirit.
Colossians 1:14	I have been redeemed and forgiven of all my sins.
Colossians 2:10	I am complete in Christ.

I AM SECURE

Romans 8:1,2	I am free from condemnation.
Romans 8:28	I am assured that all things work together for good.
Romans 8:31-34	I am free from any condemning charges against us.
Romans 8:35-39	I cannot be separated from the love of God.
2 Corinthians 1:21,22	I have been established, anointed, and sealed by God.
Colossians 3:3	I am hidden with Christ in God.
Philippians 1:6	I am confident that the good work God has begun in me will be perfected.
Philippians 3:20	I am a citizen of heaven.
2 Timothy 1:7	I have not been given a spirit of fear but of power, love and a sound mind.
Hebrews 4:16	I can find grace and mercy to help in time of need.
1 John 5:18	I am born of God and the evil one cannot touch me.

I AM SIGNIFICANT

Matthew 5:13,14	I am the salt and light of the earth.
John 15:1,5	I am a branch of the true vine, a channel of His life.
John 15:16	I have been chosen and appointed to bear fruit.
Acts 1:8	I am a personal witness of Christ.
1 Corinthians 3:16	I am God's temple.
2 Corinthians 5:17ff.	I am a minister of reconciliation for God.
2 Corinthians 6:1	I am God's coworker.
Ephesians 2:6	I am seated with Christ in the heavenly realm.
Ephesians 2:10	I am God's workmanship.
Ephesians 3:12	I may approach God with freedom and confidence.
Philippians 4:13	I can do all things through Christ who strengthens me.

Freedom in Christ Resources

Part One: *Resolving Personal Conflicts*

Victory Over the Darkness
by Neil Anderson

Start here! This is the first best-seller that along with *The Bondage Breaker* will show you how to find your freedom in Christ. Realize the power of your identity in Christ.

Paper $10 • 245 pp. B001
Study Guide • Paper $9 • 139 pp. G001

Living Free in Christ
by Neil Anderson

Based on the inspirational "Who Am I?" list from *Victory Over the Darkness*, here are 36 powerful chapters and prayers that will transform your life and dramatically show how Christ meets all of your deepest needs!

Paper $13 • 310 pp. B008

Daily in Christ
by Neil and Joanne Anderson

This uplifting 365 day devotional will encourage, motivate and challenge you to live *Daily in Christ*. There's a one-page devotional and brief heart-felt prayer for each day. Celebrate and experience your freedom all year.

Hard $17 • 365 pp. B010

Breaking Through to Spiritual Maturity
by Neil Anderson

This is a dynamic Group Study of *Victory Over the Darkness* and *The Bondage Breaker*. Complete with teaching notes for a 13 week (or 26 week) Bible study, with reproducible handouts. Ideal for Sunday school classes, Bible studies, and discipleship groups.

Paper $15 • 151 pp. G003

Resolving Personal Conflicts
by Neil Anderson

This series covers the first half of Dr. Anderson's exciting conference. Learn the truth about who you are in Christ, how to renew your mind, heal damaged emotions and truly forgive others (Part 1 of a 2-part series).

Video Tape Set $95 • 8 lessons V001
Audio Tape Set $40 • 8 lessons A001
Additional workbooks $4 • Paper 32 pp. W001

Resolving Spiritual Conflicts & Cross-Cultural Ministry
by Dr. Timothy Warner

This series has powerful lessons on missions, world view and warfare relationships that are extremely helpful for every Christian. It provides key insights for spiritual growth and ministry.

Video Tape Set $85 • 8 lessons V005
Audio Tape Set $35 • 8 lessons A005
Additional workbooks $4 • paper 47 pp. W005

Part Two: *Resolving Spiritual Conflicts*

The Bondage Breaker
by Neil Anderson

This best-seller shares the definitive process of breaking bond-ages and the *Steps to Freedom in Christ*. Read this with *Victory Over the Darkness* and you will be able to resolve your personal and spiritual conflicts.

Paper $10 • 247 pp. B002
Study Guide • Paper $6 • 121 pp. G002

The Steps to Freedom in Christ
by Neil Anderson

This is a handy version of the *Steps to Freedom in Christ*, the Discipleship Counseling process from *The Bondage Breaker*. It is ideal for personal use or for helping another person who wants to find his freedom.

Paper $2 • 19 pp. G004

The Steps to Freedom in Christ Video
with Dr. Neil Anderson

In this special video experience, Dr. Neil Anderson personally leads you or a loved one through the bondage-breaking Steps to Freedom in Christ in the privacy of your living room. Includes The Steps to Freedom in Christ booklet.

Video $19.99 • 70 minutes • UPC 607135.002550

Spiritual Warfare
by Dr. Timothy Warner

This concise book offers balanced, biblical insights on spiritual warfare with practical information and ammunition for winning the spiritual battle. Every reader will benefit by learning from the author's extensive experience.

Paper $9 • 160 pp. B007

Resolving Spiritual Conflicts
by Neil Anderson

This series offers the second half of Dr. Anderson's exciting conference. Every believer needs to fully understand his position, authority and protection in Christ, and the enemy's tactics (Part 2 of a 2-part series).

Video Tape Set $95 • 8 lessons V002
Audio Tape Set $40 • 8 lessons A002
Additional workbooks $4 • Paper 49 pp. W002

Freedom in Christ Resources

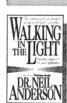

Freedom in Christ Resources

Parenting Resources

Spiritual Protection for Your Children
by Neil Anderson and Peter and Sue Vanderhook

The fascinating true story of a average middle-class American family's spiritual battle on the home front and the lessons we can all learn about protecting our families from the enemy's attacks.

Hardcover $19 • 300 pp. B021

The Seduction of Our Children
by Neil Anderson and Steve Russo

A battle is raging for the minds of our children. It's a battle parents <u>must</u> win. This timely book will prepare parents to counter the world's assault against their families. Includes helpful prayers for children of various ages.

Paper $9 • 245 pp. B004

The Seduction of Our Children
by Neil Anderson

This parenting series will change the way you view the spiritual development of your children. Helpful insights are offered on many parenting issues, such as discipline, communication and spiritual oversight of children. A panel of experts share their advice.

Video Tape Set $85 • 6 lessons V002
Audio Tape Set #35 • 6 lessons A002
Additional workbooks $4 • 49 pp. W002

Youth Resources

Stomping Out the Darkness
by Neil Anderson and Dave Park

This youth version of *Victory Over the Darkness* shows youth how to break free and dis-cover the joy of their identity in Christ (Part 1 of 2).

Paper $9 • 210 pp. B102
Study Guide Paper $8 • 137 pp. G101

The Bondage Breaker Youth Edition
by Neil Anderson and Dave Park

This youth best-seller shares the process of breaking bondages and the *Youth Steps to Freedom in Christ*. Read this with *Stomping Out the Darkness* (Part 2 of 2). **Paper $8 • 227 pp. B102**
Study Guide Paper $6 • 128 pp. G102

Busting Free!
by Neil Anderson and Dave Park

This is a dynamic Group Study of *Stomping Out the Darkness* and *The Bondage Breaker Youth Edition*. It has complete teaching notes for a 13 week (or 26 week) Bible study, with reproducible hand-outs. Ideal for Sunday school classes, Bible studies, and youth discipleship groups of all kinds. **Paper $17 • 163 pp. G103**

Youth Topics

Helping Young People Find Freedom in Christ
by Neil Anderson and Rich Miller

This youth version provides comprehensive, hands-on biblical Discipleship Counseling training for youth workers and youth pastors, equipping them to help young people. This resource is Part 3 continuing from the message of Parts 1 and 2.

Paper $13 • 300 pp. B112

Know Light, No Fear
by Neil Anderson and Rich Miller

In this youth version of *Walking in the Light* young people learn how to know God's will for their lives. They will discover key truths about divine guidance and helpful warnings for avoiding spiritual counterfeits.

Paper $10 • 250 pp. B111

Purity Under Pressure
by Neil Anderson and Dave Park

Real answers for real world pressures! Youth will find out the difference between being friends, dating, and having a relationship. No hype, no big lectures, just straightforward talk about living free in Christ.

Paper $8 • 200 pp. B104

To My Dear Slimeball
by Rich Miller

In the spirit of C. S. Lewis' *Screwtape Letters*, this humorous story, filled with biblical truth, is an allegory of the spiritual battle every believer faces. Discover how 15-year-old David's life is amazingly similar to your own.

Paper $8 each • 250 pp. B103

Youth Devotionals

These four devotionals help young people understand God's love and their identity in Christ. Teens will learn to establish a positive spiritual habit of getting into God's Word on a daily basis.

Extreme Faith
Paper $8
204 pp. B106

Reality Check
Paper $8
200 pp. B107

Awesome God
Paper $8
200 pp. B108

Ultimate Love
Paper $8
200 pp. B109

How Freedom in Christ Resources Work Together

This chart shows "at a glance" how Freedom in Christ's resources interrelate and their correct order of progression from basic to advanced.

Part One

THIS IS FREEDOM IN CHRIST'S CORE MESSAGE OF RESOLVING PERSONAL AND SPIRITUAL CONFLICTS

- *Victory Over the Darkness*
- *Victory Over the Darkness Study Guide*
- *Living Free in Christ*
- *Daily in Christ*

Part Two

- *The Bondage Breaker*
- *The Bondage Breaker Study Guide*
- *Steps to Freedom in Christ*
- *Spiritual Warfare*
- *Breaking Through to Spiritual Maturity Teaching Guide*
  (Covers parts 1 and 2)

"Resolving Personal and Spiritual Conflicts" Conference and Audios/Videos
(Covers parts 1 and 2)

"Resolving Spiritual Conflicts and Cross-cultural Ministry" Conference and Audios/Videos
(Covers parts 1 and 2)

"Shepherd's Time Out" Conference
(Covers parts 1, 2 and 3)

"If you hold to My teaching, you are really My disciples. Then you will know the truth, and the truth will set you free."

Part Three

PRACTICAL BIBLICAL ANSWERS FOR DISCIPLESHIP COUNSELING

- *Helping Others Find Freedom in Christ*
- *Helping Others Find Freedom in Christ Training Manual and Study Guide*
- *Released From Bondage*
- *Freedom From Addiction*

"Spiritual Conflicts and Counseling" Audios/Videos

"Helping Others Find Freedom in Christ" Video Training Program

"Church Leadership and Discipleship Counseling" Conference

"Freedom From Addiction" Conference and Video Study

Part Four

CHURCH LEADERSHIP

- *Setting Your Church Free*
- *Steps to Setting Your Church Free*

"Setting Your Church Free" Conference and Audios/Videos

Topical

- *Walking in the Light*
- *A Way of Escape*
- *The Common Made Holy*
- *The Christ-Centered Marriage*
- *Spiritual Protection for Your Children*
- *The Seduction of Our Children*

"The Christ-Centered Marriage" Conference and Audios/Videos

"The Seduction of Our Children" Conference and Audios/Videos

Contact Freedom in Christ at:

491 E. Lambert Road
La Habra, CA 90631-6136
Phone: (562) 691-9128
Fax (562) 691-4035

World Wide Web:
www.freedominchrist.com

Email:
73430.2630@compuserve.com

See separate chart for youth or young adult resources!